THE MINISTRY OF PLEASURE

Craig Baxter

The Ministry of Pleasure

OBERON BOOKS
LONDON

First published in 2004 by Oberon Books Ltd
(incorporating Absolute Classics)
521 Caledonian Road, London N7 9RH
Tel: 020 7607 3637 / Fax: 020 7607 3629
e-mail: oberon.books@btinternet.com
www.oberonbooks.com

A catalogue record for this book is available from the British
Library.

ISBN: 1 84002 491 7

Cover image by Ben Pacey (www.doublebee.co.uk), from a
drawing by Aubrey Beardsley.

Characters

JOHN WILMOT, EARL OF ROCHESTER

ANNE, COUNTESS OF ROCHESTER, his mother

ELIZABETH MALET

SIR JOHN WARRE, her stepfather

LORD HAWLEY, her grandfather

EARL OF MULGRAVE, her suitor

KING CHARLES II

QUEEN CATHARINE, his wife

BARBARA CASTLEMAINE, his mistress

JANE ROBERTS, a Court beauty

WILLIAM FANSHAWE, a wealthy gentleman

NELL, an actress

TOM, an actor

THOMAS WYNDHAM, a dead gentleman sailor

EDWARD MONTAGU, a dead gentleman sailor

MRS TASKER, a brothel madam

GILBERT BURNET, a cleric

WILLIAM CHIFFINCH, the Palace gatekeeper

SERVANT

SEXTON

HOODED ACCOMPLICES

GAOLER

SOLDIERS

ROYAL COUNCILLORS

PROSTITUTES

MADAME FOURCARD, a poxhouse madam

TAVERN DRINKERS

5

The first performance of *The Ministry of Pleasure* took place at the Latchmere Theatre, London, on 9 June 2004, with the following cast:

ROCHESTER, Martin Delaney

ELIZABETH , Frida Show

KING, Johnnie Lyne-Pirkis

ANNE / BARBARA, Charlotte Fields

QUEEN / JANE / NELL, Amy Humphreys

FANSHAWE / SIR JOHN / MRS TASKER,
Neil Summerville

MULGRAVE / WYNDHAM, Sean Patterson

BURNET / HAWLEY / SERVANT / TOM /
MONTAGU / CHIFFINCH, Robert Gillespie

Additional roles distributed amongst the cast.

Director, Stuart Mullins
Designer, Jeremy Daker
Lighting, Phil Hewitt
Composer, Simon McCorry
Assistant Director, Will Hammond

The play covers the time from John Wilmot, Earl of Rochester's arrival at the English Court of Charles II in 1664 until his death.

The author would like to thank the following people who helped with the development of this script: Cathy Ashbee, David Carter, Rick Harvey, Matt McConaghy, Joseph Millson, Matthew Morrison, Stuart Mullins, Jeremy Webb, Tom Williams and the Latchmere Production Team.

Part One

Scene 1 – Telescope

Privy Gardens, Whitehall Palace: KING
The KING sets up his newest toy – a telescope – and aims it at the
sky. Beside the telescope are pen, ink and paper for taking notes.

Scene 2 – Restoration

Graveside, Oxfordshire: ROCHESTER; ANNE; BURNET;
SEXTON
ROCHESTER, ANNE and the Revd Dr BURNET watch as the
SEXTON struggles painfully slowly to shovel soil on top of the coffin
in a grave. It's painful to watch. ROCHESTER holds a letter.
BURNET breaks the uncomfortable silence.

BURNET: Will you be going to serve the King, My Lord,
  like your father before you?

ROCHESTER: I will. In fact, since I've letters for His
  Majesty from the Duchess of Orléans, I need to leave as
  soon as our business here is concluded.

ANNE: Go then, if you must.

ROCHESTER: Mother.

ANNE: But do not forget your first duty is to God. It is
  God who has blessed you with your great gifts. I warn
  you: the people you will meet at Court, though neat and
  gay in their apparel, are brutish, rough, rude,
  whoremongers, vain, empty, careless. I know you wish to
  make your mark with your King. And you father would
  have wished it so. He loved his King. But remember:
  your duty is to God. Kings are not what we once
  believed them to be. So go to him. Honour him. Do
  your duty by him. But do not forsake your prayers.

ROCHESTER impatient at having to listen to yet another of his mother's sermons and of watching the slow progress of the SEXTON steps up to the grave.

ROCHESTER: Give me that.

SEXTON: My Lord?

ROCHESTER: The shovel. Hold these. (*The letters.*)

ROCHESTER takes up the shovel and proceeds to fill in the grave. The SEXTON holds the Duchess's letters.

SEXTON: I knew your father as a boy My Lord.

ROCHESTER: You're more fortunate than I.

SEXTON: Liked his drink.

ROCHESTER: His drink too is more fortunate than I.

ANNE: Thank you for conducting the service Dr Burnet.

BURNET: You said you wanted nothing too sentimental.

ANNE: It was entirely appropriate

SEXTON: How long's he been dead?

ROCHESTER: He's been eight years in an exile's grave near Bruges.

SEXTON: Not too much left of him by now, I shouldn't wonder.

ROCHESTER: You're right, you probably shouldn't.

The SEXTON, ANNE and BURNET watch ROCHESTER complete the job.

SEXTON: Good Oxfordshire soil that.

ROCHESTER tramps the dirt down with his boot.

ANNE: Thank you John. For bringing him home.

ROCHESTER: The King has had his restoration, now we have ours.

ROCHESTER takes the letters back from the SEXTON and hands him back the shovel.

Scene 3 – Comet

Privy Gardens (evening): KING; QUEEN; BARBARA; ROCHESTER; FANSHAWE
KING CHARLES II is showing QUEEN CATHARINE the night sky through his telescope. He speaks no Portuguese; she speaks only basic English.

KING: ... Aristotelians will dribble on about 'combustible emanations arising from the earth to the region of fire above the sky.' The feeling at the Royal Society, however, is –

QUEEN: Onde está o cometa? *(Where is the comet?)*

KING: What?

QUEEN: Where?

KING: Up there. See?

QUEEN: Ah.

KING: The feeling at the Royal Society is rather that the origin of comets is astral.

QUEEN: What mean?

KING: They come down from up there rather than up from down here.

BARBARA arrives, the KING and she exchanging smirks.

QUEEN: Is good or is bad?

KING: What?

QUEEN: Is good or is bad?

KING: Is comet. Good or bad don't come into it. Is comet. Barbara, have you seen the comet?

QUEEN: Is comet. Is beautiful?

KING: Is ice. Or is fire. Or is dust. You cannot see with the naked eye, but through these magnifying lenses you may observe its possession of a tail.

QUEEN: Like a little dog? Or a monkey tail?

BARBARA: Your Majesty, the Earl of Rochester is here to see you. Henry Wilmot's son.

KING: The son, of course, of course.

BARBARA: He's returned from an 'educational tour' of Europe with a letter for you from your sister.

ROCHESTER has entered, holding the letters.

KING: You have your father's complexion Rochester.

ROCHESTER: (*Bowing.*) Your Majesty.

KING: Your father and I, as I'm sure you know, were fugitives together after the Battle of Worcester.

BARBARA: (*Gently mocking.*) 'On the run, hiding in treetops, sheltered by the loyal heart of Englishmen and women.'

KING: I'm over-fond of telling the tale.

ROCHESTER: I've brought my father's body back to England. He's at rest now in Spelsbury. As I said to my mother: the King has had his restoration and now we have ours.

KING: (*ROCHESTER's remark falling flat, he changes the subject*) You've letters from my sister?

ROCHESTER: I have.

ROCHESTER hands over the letters. Immediately, the KING breaks open the seal and reads.

BARBARA: So, My Lord, how was Oxfordshire when you left it?

ROCHESTER: Damp, green and full of cows, Your Royal Highness. I don't care greatly for the country.

BARBARA: (*Tickled pink.*) Oh no, you're mistaken I'm afraid. I'm not Her Royal Highness. I'm married to the Earl of Castlemaine. You and I are cousins, I believe, on your mother's side. This is Her Royal Highness the Queen.

QUEEN: Please to meet you. You are in Rochester yes? Hiding up in the big oak tree yes?

ROCHESTER: (*Mortified.*) Your Royal Highness.

BARBARA: I do partake of certain of her privileges, however.

QUEEN: I understand.

BARBARA: Her English is improving all the time.

QUEEN: I understand, you think I don't, what happen.

The KING wanders off, re-reading his letters. The QUEEN and BARBARA follow him. When ROCHESTER goes to follow also, BARBARA stops him with a gesture – his audience is over.

KING: Always, her letters frustrate me with their brevity. Though she makes pains to speak well of Young Rochester. He must have made an impression. An 'eloquent fellow with a drink inside him' it seems. Take him in hand. We need more of his kind here. Young men of spunk and sparkle.

BARBARA: It would be a pleasure.

KING: I am certain it would.

The KING, QUEEN and BARBARA exit, leaving ROCHESTER alone at a loss what to do next. He takes a look through the telescope. Suddenly inspired, he takes up the pen beside it and starts to write. Engrossed, he does not notice the arrival of the foppish FANSHAWE, who carries a bottle of red wine and a glass from which he liberally drinks.

FANSHAWE: Another country cavalier come to claim the King owes him a living I assume.

ROCHESTER: The King and my father were the best of friends.

FANSHAWE: His Majesty is excellent at making friends. Has to be in his position. I wouldn't bother with any of that (*ROCHESTER's writings.*) you know. Everyone these days thinks they're a damn poet. His Majesty has no need for more poets or politicians. Many too many of those here already.

ROCHESTER: (*Acknowledging the telescope.*) He's more interested in astrology?

FANSHAWE: Astronomy please. The last man to cast his horoscope, he cast into the Tower. No, the King is a man of science. You know I heard him say the other day that the World rotates about the Sun.

ROCHESTER: Everyone knows that to be true.

FANSHAWE: But the sun rises in the West, circles overhead and sets at dusk in the East.

ROCHESTER: It sets in the West. Rises in the East.

FANSHAWE: Exactly: science. Marvellous. By the way your shoes are appalling. You must get yourself a pair of something decent. You'll never amount to anything in those. Here, take a drink. (*Puts the bottle down on the table in front of ROCHESTER.*) Enjoy your time here while it lasts. I've no doubt you'll be packed off back to wherever it is you came from before you know it.

With a belch, FANSHAWE wanders off. ROCHESTER looks down and seems suddenly unimpressed by his poetry. He screws it up and throws it away. He picks up the red wine bottle and swigs deeply from it.

Scene 4 – King Charles' spaniel

Palace Interior (evening): ROCHESTER; MULGRAVE; FANSHAWE; JANE; BARBARA; KING

ROCHESTER wanders through the Palace, increasingly inebriated. As music strikes up, he watches BARBARA, FANSHAWE, MULGRAVE and JANE ROBERTS come together for a dance.

JANE: Where's His Majesty this evening?

MULGRAVE: In his laboratory.

JANE: What does he do in his laboratory?

FANSHAWE: You wouldn't wish to know.

BARBARA: He's dissecting a rat.

JANE: Is that a type of dance?

BARBARA: Not exactly.

JANE: 'Dissecting a rat'?

MULGRAVE: It's like a public execution but on a smaller scale.

JANE: He's executing rats?

FANSHAWE: And examining their entrails.

JANE: Why would he want to execute a rat?

MULGRAVE: He's the King. He does as he pleases.

JANE: Not always.

BARBARA: Is it true Mistress Roberts, that you are the last virgin left in the whole of England?

JANE: Surely Lady Castlemaine does not envy my humble virtue?

BARBARA: Not for one moment. Like everyone else here, I find it immensely tedious.

FANSHAWE: Chastity is an over-rated virtue

JANE: I intend to remain a virgin all my life and never to become tedious.

BARBARA and FANSHAWE yawn in unison.

ROCHESTER, by now very pissed, decides to intervene in proceedings.

MULGRAVE: Who the devil is that?

BARBARA: That is the Earl of Rochester.

FANSHAWE: The King and his father were best of friends, apparently.

MULGRAVE: Look at the state of him.

FANSHAWE: I know, the shoes are unspeakable.

ROCHESTER stumbles into the middle of the dance, and falls over. The music and the dancing stop and all eyes are on him. He picks himself up off the floor, laughing.

BARBARA: What is it that you find so amusing, My Lord?

ROCHESTER milks his moment.

ROCHESTER: I've just watched two of the King's dogs shagging under a table.

MULGRAVE: And why should that be of any interest to us? There are ladies present, in case you hadn't noticed.

ROCHESTER: And one of them has shat in the fireplace.

FANSHAWE: Ladies! I am shocked.

BABRARA No, I'm certain that too would have been one of the dogs.

JANE: It's true! I noticed a turd in the grate earlier myself. I didn't like to mention it.

Everyone except MULGRAVE is enjoying the conversation. Then ROCHESTER starts to scurry about on all fours, yapping like a dog at the ladies' ankles. JANE and the BARBARA seem delighted.

JANE: Charades!

BARBARA: You have Brunhilda off to a tee.

JANE: Get away from me you dreadful hound!

ROCHESTER rolls over for JANE and she tickles his tummy.

MULGRAVE: My Lord, you are humiliating yourself and embarrassing the ladies.

ROCHESTER growls at him.

MULGRAVE: I have heard it said that Rochester's boy was something of a jumped-up pup. However, I never imagined it was meant quite so literally.

ROCHESTER: And I have heard it said, Sir...

MULGRAVE: Lord.

ROCHESTER: Lord...?

MULGRAVE: Mulgrave.

ROCHESTER: ...across the continent, that the restored English Court is the place to be. In France, they say that after Charles the First and the national tragedy of Cromwell, Charlie Two is the most exquisite comedy.

Unseen by all, the KING has entered.

And comedy it is. I can see why, in the end, everyone gets bored, gets married, and goes off to live in the country. None of you here seems actually to know how to enjoy yourself. You don't drink enough.

FANSHAWE: Untrue!

ROCHESTER: Apart from Fanshawe here. (*Grabs JANE about the waist.*) You don't eat enough. You don't laugh. You don't fuck enough. You don't celebrate life like they do in France and Italy! You stand to one side of it, sneering and sniggering at it, fretting about the latest fashions and doing your poncy dances. The King's dogs and horses have a better time, doing as they truly please.

KING: Well Rochester...

A collective gasp. ROCHESTER freezes. All heads turn to the KING.

MULGRAVE: This dog has had his day.

KING: What do you propose doing about it?

ROCHESTER: (*Improvising with increasing confidence.*) Your Majesty, I propose, for your delight and edification…an experiment in living! A scientific investigation of every possible cause and source of worldly enjoyment. I will report, in detail, all my findings, within both the animal and the human sphere, and direct to His Majesty, that he may properly educate his court and his subjects in the attainment of perfect pleasure.

KING: (*Giving nothing away as to whether he is angry or amused.*) We will discuss your proposal further in the morning, when you are sober. Join me for tennis at eight o'clock. My apologies for interrupting, everyone, please continue with your…whatever it was that you were doing.

The KING leaves. No one else knows quite what to do. The music starts up again half-heartedly.

Scene 5 – Real tennis I

Real Tennis Court (morning): KING; ROCHESTER
The KING (confidently) and ROCHESTER (struggling) play tennis.

KING: I need to speak to you about money Wilmot.

ROCHESTER returns a shot (just).

That's it. Well done.

The KING returns his shot with ease.

We need to find some way to fund your great experiment. What's your annual pension?

ROCHESTER fluffs his shot.

ROCHESTER: Sorry?

KING: Your annual pension, what's it worth?

ROCHESTER: Five hundred pounds. The estate my father left us was not –

KING: Five hundred pounds is not enough to keep you here.

ROCHESTER: I see.

KING: If I could support you myself, I would. But I owe too much to too many people. I've barely enough in the coffers to pay for tennis balls. I'm being open with you here.

ROCHESTER: It's appreciated.

KING: I can't afford to keep you. At least not without it being to the detriment of some other gentleman. And I'm not in the business of making enemies.

ROCHESTER: Except with the Dutch?

KING: (*After a smile.*) However.

ROCHESTER: However?

KING: There is an heiress in town worth, so I hear, twenty five hundred pounds per annum. Her name is Elizabeth Malet, and word is she has a fine figure and a not unpleasant face. In the absence of a father, I would be prepared to recommend you to her guardians…you look dismayed.

ROCHESTER: I hadn't thought to marry quite so –

KING: I think you'll find marriage to be a most agreeable state, particularly when you are in Town and she is in the Country, particularly when she has estates and money. I've written you a letter of recommendation.

The KING hands ROCHESTER a letter.

Meet her first, then decide. If she offends your eye, think of her money. If she enchants you, then follow your passion. There's nothing to be lost and everything to gain: think of the experiment. Now, forty-love, I make it.

The KING serves. ROCHESTER stands holding his letter.

Scene 6 – Elizabeth

Sir John Warre's house (morning): SIR JOHN; HAWLEY; ELIZABETH; MULGRAVE; ROCHESTER
ROCHESTER, in the background, has found an uncorked bottle of wine and pours himself an enormous glassful. He observes, unseen, the following interchange and is pleasantly surprised to find himself immediately attracted to ELIZABETH. Inspired, he gets out pen and paper and writes, looking up from time to time to watch ELIZABETH.

SIR JOHN: The good news is we now have firm interest from Sir William Fanshawe.

ELIZABETH is more interested in unpeeling and eating her orange.

HAWLEY: Who's the fellow we're seeing now?

SIR JOHN: Mulgrave.

HAWLEY: He's the son of whatsisname?

SIR JOHN: The Earl of Mulgrave.

HAWLEY: And whose son is Fanshawe?

SIR JOHN: Ormonde.

HAWLEY: The Duke of?

SIR JOHN: The Duke thereof, indeed.

ELIZABETH: I won't marry him if he's ugly.

HAWLEY: What?

ELIZABETH: I said I won't marry him if he's ugly. Or tedious.

HAWLEY: How dare you speak with so disrespectful a tone!

ELIZABETH: Or old.

HAWLEY: Do you persist with this idiocy? Do you think you may marry whomsoever you choose? Do you imagine your stepfather and I are in the business of pandering to your every whim?

ELIZABETH: No, I can tell you are in the business of ignoring my every opinion and ensuring my lifelong unhappiness.

HAWLEY: Do you think, child, you may adopt tones without fear of a beating?

SIR JOHN: Elizabeth, we would not make you do that which you did not wish to do.

HAWLEY: I would! Out of sheer spite for her manner and tone, I would!

SIR JOHN: We would not make you marry whom you did not wish to marry.

HAWLEY: I would! For mine own grim amusement, I would!

SIR JOHN: We would not suggest any unsuitable gentleman.

The highly unsuitable MULGRAVE arrives to ELIZABETH's horror.

MULGRAVE: Ahem.

SIR JOHN: Lord Mulgrave?

MULGRAVE: John Sheffield, Earl of Mulgrave. Sirs. Mademoiselle.

ELIZABETH covers her mouth to smother a giggle. She attempts to leave.

ELIZABETH: My Lord, you must excuse me, I do not feel well.

SIR JOHN: But Elizabeth, this eminent Earl, no less, has travelled all this way to see you.

ELIZABETH: I'm sure neither you nor Lord Mulgrave would appreciate it were I to puke before him.

HAWLEY: You will stay here. Where are your manners girl?

MULGRAVE: You know why I am here? You received my letter?

SIR JOHN: Oh yes, we're extremely honoured that you –

HAWLEY: I know the Duke of Ormonde well.

MULGRAVE: Indeed? I've never had the good fortune of meeting him.

HAWLEY: What?

SIR JOHN: (*Whisper to HAWLEY.*) No, this is Mulgrave.

HAWLEY: Ah Mulgrave. I also know Lord Mulgrave intimately. He's your father, I believe?

MULGRAVE: I am Lord Mulgrave.

HAWLEY: So is Lord Mulgrave not your father?

MULGRAVE: Do you question my parentage?

HAWLEY: What? No, no.

MULGRAVE: If you would, in public, and before ladies, question my parentage, you will force me to consider steps towards defending the honour you seek to tarnish.

HAWLEY: Steps, steps? What's he talking about, steps?

MULGRAVE: The satisfaction of a duel, My Lord.

HAWLEY: A duel?! Nonsense. I simply said I know and admire your father, that's all, nothing more. A duel? Nonsense.

SIR JOHN: We have received your letter, My Lord, and are most honoured by your interest in my stepdaughter.

HAWLEY: My granddaughter.

SIR JOHN: I apologise if my…

HAWLEY: I apologise if I…

SIR JOHN: …inadvertently offended you.

HAWLEY: Indeed yes.

SIR JOHN: He was momentarily confused as to…

HAWLEY: I was momentarily confused as to…um.

MULGRAVE: Well uh…

SIR JOHN: (*After a pause.*) Here she stands. Elizabeth. On her mother's death, she will receive per annum the sum of twenty five hundred pounds. I see you are impressed. We are a well-connected family, though far less distinguished, of course, than your own.

HAWLEY: She's a respectful girl…

ELIZABETH sticks her tongue out at HAWLEY.

…and not unattractive.

MULGRAVE: How is her mother?

SIR JOHN: She is / well.

HAWLEY: She is ill.

SIR JOHN: She is as well as can be expected of one so ill. It's kind of you to ask.

MULGRAVE: I would appreciate an opportunity to become better acquainted with her.

SIR JOHN: You would?

MULGRAVE: The daughter I mean.

SIR JOHN: Naturally.

HAWLEY: Little point with her mother, seeing as –

SIR JOHN: Have you dined this evening?

MULGRAVE: I have.

SIR JOHN: Ah. I was about to suggest that we, all of us, dined together this evening.

MULGRAVE: But I have dined already.

SIR JOHN: Would you care to dine again?

MULGRAVE: I would not.

SIR JOHN: Ah.

MULGRAVE: Would Thursday next be convenient?

SIR JOHN: Thursday next, yes. We do have, as you might imagine, other interested parties –

MULGRAVE: Would Thursday next be convenient or not?

HAWLEY: Yes!

SIR JOHN: Thursday next would be most convenient.

MULGRAVE: I will have sent to you word of time and venue. Good day.

MULGRAVE exits.
In the background, ROCHESTER has tucked the poem he is composing in a pocket and has topped-up the wine glass.

HAWLEY: Good day!

SIR JOHN: Good day!

ELIZABETH: Good God.

HAWLEY: Seemed a nice enough fellow.

SIR JOHN: First rate credentials.

ELIZABETH: Would anyone care to know what I thought of Lord Mulgrave?

HAWLEY: / No!

SIR JOHN: Of course.

ELIZABETH huffs off but across her path is ROCHESTER, holding his letter from the KING in one hand and an enormous glass of claret (which he has poured from a bottle of SIR JOHN's) in the other.

ROCHESTER: Escaping...

ELIZABETH is startled to come across ROCHESTER but quickly recovers her dignity.

...from someone?

ELIZABETH: I wasn't escaping.

ROCHESTER: Why not?

ELIZABETH: There's nowhere to escape to.

ROCHESTER offers the claret.

ROCHESTER: There's oblivion.

ELIZABETH: Is that my stepfather's wine?

ROCHESTER: I found a bottle open in the hall. I assumed it was for guests.

ELIZABETH: Guests and intruders. Which are you?

ELIZABETH takes the claret and drinks deeply.

ROCHESTER: Both, neither. An unexpected guest. (*A request for a swig.*) You wouldn't want to travel all the way to oblivion alone?

ELIZABETH: That depends on the company.

ELIZABETH hands ROCHESTER the glass.

ROCHESTER: Oblivion is never as pleasurable as the journey there?

ROCHESTER drinks deeply.

ELIZABETH: Make sure you enjoy the journey: it's expensive wine.

ELIZABETH takes back the glass and polishes off the wine.

ELIZABETH: So you are not expected?

ROCHESTER: And neither, I must confess, were you. I take it you are Elizabeth Malet?

ELIZABETH: And you are –?

ROCHESTER: John Wilmot, Earl of Rochester. Will you marry me?

ELIZABETH stares at ROCHESTER.
SIR JOHN WARRE and LORD HAWLEY bluster upon them, shocked to find ELIZABETH alone with a stranger.

HAWLEY: What!?

SIR JOHN: Elizabeth?

HAWLEY: What!?

SIR JOHN: Has this gentleman…? Is he…? What…?

HAWLEY: What!?

ELIZABETH: He has asked me to marry him.

HAWLEY: Aha!

ROCHESTER casually picks up an orange.

ROCHESTER: I await My Lady's reply.

ELIZABETH: It was an extremely abrupt proposal.

ROCHESTER: Direct, but from the heart, I do assure you.

SIR JOHN: You cannot…I cannot allow you to…I fear you cannot simply ask Elizabeth to marry you, Sir. Everything must be done through us, her guardians, in the proper fashion.

HAWLEY: What's that in your hand, Sir?

ROCHESTER: An orange, Sir.

HAWLEY: Did you offer him an orange, Miss?

ELIZABETH: I did not.

HAWLEY: Are you stealing fruit, Sir?

ROCHESTER: I –

HAWLEY: You are a thief. What's your name, Sir?

ROCHESTER: Rochester.

HAWLEY: Rochester?

ROCHESTER: John Wilmot, Earl of Rochester, Sir.

SIR JOHN: A lord?

HAWLEY: A very *minor* lord.

SIR JOHN: I knew your father.

HAWLEY: I knew your father, he was an idiot, Sir. What do you say to that? I said: what do you say to that?

ROCHESTER: I'm told I more resemble my mother in both looks and temperament.

HAWLEY: Do you seriously imagine we would consider you fit to marry my granddaughter? Do you know who she is? Do you know what she is worth? You – a minor lord. A stealer of fruit!

ROCHESTER: I've a letter from the King.

SIR JOHN: (*Impressed.*) From the King?

ROCHESTER: To Lord Hawley and Sir John Warre.

HAWLEY: From the King?

SIR JOHN: Let me see.

SIR JOHN and HAWLEY read the letter.

ROCHESTER: (*to Elizabeth*) What's your answer?

SIR JOHN: Don't! Don't speak to him Elizabeth. Wait please, until…

ELIZABETH: (*Playful.*) I've nothing whatever to say to him.

SIR JOHN: Good.

SIR JOHN and HAWLEY continue to read the letter. ROCHESTER begins to tuck into the orange. He offers a segment to ELIZABETH, which she takes and eats.

HAWLEY: (*To SIR JOHN.*) It's a good letter.

SIR JOHN: The King speaks well of you, My Lord.

ROCHESTER: The King and my father were close friends.

HAWLEY: I knew your father, he was…

ROCHESTER: He was an idiot, you have said.

HAWLEY: No no no no. Not at all.

SIR JOHN: If you don't mind my cutting to the quick, My Lord, what exactly is your value? Your income?

ROCHESTER: Five hundred a year.

SIR JOHN's eyes immediately glaze over. He plucks the letter from HAWLEY's hand and passes it back to ROCHESTER.

SIR JOHN: Thank you, Sir, your interest has been noted.

ROCHESTER: (*To ELIZABETH.*) You haven't yet given me an answer?

SIR JOHN: Of course, we will consider your proposal, but you understand my stepdaughter's financial well-being must be our prime concern. Now you must excuse us, we have much to do and we're dining later at the Palace. Elizabeth?

ELIZABETH crosses to her stepfather and grandfather, still playing it very cool. Unseen by SIR JOHN and HAWLEY, ROCHESTER presses his poem into ELIZABETH's hand as she walks past him.

ELIZABETH: My Lord.

SIR JOHN: Good day.

HAWLEY: Sir.

SIR JOHN, HAWLEY and ELIZABETH leave ROCHESTER in their wake. ELIZABETH is already reading ROCHESTER's poem.

ROCHESTER: 'Since first my dazzled eyes were thrown on that bewitching face...'

ELIZABETH: '...like ruined birds robbed of their young. Lamenting, frighted and alone....'

ROCHESTER departs.

HAWLEY: What's that you're reading Missy?

ELIZABETH: A friend's talk of the season's flowers. It's very trivial.

HAWLEY: Sounds it. (*To SIR JOHN.*) Who's the fellow we're seeing next?

SIR JOHN: Lord John Butler.

HAWLEY: Ormonde's boy?

SIR JOHN: Sandwich's.

ELIZABETH: '...I fly from place to place. My rifled love would soon retire, dissolving into air...'

Scene 7 – Real tennis II

Real Tennis Court (morning): KING; ROCHESTER; BARBARA; MULGRAVE
ROCHESTER and the KING play tennis again. This time the game is more even.
ROCHESTER hits a ball with confidence.

ROCHESTER: '...should I that nymph cease to admire. Blest in whose arms I will expire.'

The KING, at full stretch returns ROCHESTER's shot into the net.

'...or at her feet despair.'

KING: (*Irritated to have lost the point.*) A sweet poem. Though barely credible in its sentiment. I hope you're doing more than writing second-rate poetry to secure her hand.

ROCHESTER: (*A lie.*) Of course.

KING: Do you intend to serve?

Out of earshot of the KING and ROCHESTER, MULGRAVE complains to BARBARA.

MULGRAVE: He's playing him again.

BARBARA: Perhaps they are well matched.

MULGRAVE: But one is the King and the other a jumped-up little shit. Forgive my language but it cannot be right.

BARBARA: I meant perhaps their games are evenly matched. How's your tennis?

MULGRAVE: First rate.

BARBARA: Well you offer him a game.

MULGRAVE: I have.

BARBARA: Perhaps His Majesty is too concerned that you will beat him.

MULGRAVE: But the King must win.

BARBARA: Why's that?

MULGRAVE: The King must always win. That is the necessary order of things.

ROCHESTER wins the point and the game. He beams.

ROCHESTER: Game to me, I think.

KING: Really? I wasn't keeping score.

BARBARA steps on to the tennis court.

BARBARA: Your Majesty.

KING: Barbara, is it time?

BARBARA: I believe it is. Rochester, come. You and I have work to do for His Majesty. We shall see you in your laboratory shortly.

KING: Excellent.

BARBARA leads ROCHESTER away.

MULGRAVE: Might I accompany His Majesty to his laboratory?

KING: For what purpose?

MULGRAVE: I've long been fascinated by all things scientific.

KING: Why then of course Mulgrave. Step this way.

Scene 8 – Microscope

Laboratory (day): KING; MULGRAVE; BARBARA; ROCHESTER; JANE; ELIZABETH; SIR JOHN; HAWLEY The KING encourages MULGRAVE to look down the microscope at a slide he has prepared. As the KING brings it into focus, MULGRAVE jumps at what he sees.

MULGRAVE: Eugh. What is that!?

KING: A flea.

MULGRAVE: Where did you find such a creature, Your Majesty?

KING: On a rat.

MULGRAVE: What size was the rat?!

KING: It was of standard proportions, as is this flea. But observed through these magnifying lenses, it appears many times its true size.

MULGRAVE: What a remarkable toy.

KING: It's not a toy, Mulgrave. It's a scientific instrument.

MULGRAVE: I meant no disrespect.

KING: A key for unlocking the secrets of the Universe.

MULGRAVE: Who'd've imagined the workings of a flea to be so intricate?

KING: Not you, evidently. But every day now there are new worlds discovered. We're seeing things that were, before, invisible: the rings of Saturn; the stardust tails of comets; flecks of black upon the sun; the pumping heart; the fleas that live on fleas. Feats of engineering surpassing those of the greatest clockmaker. The flea is revealed as a wonder of creation. And before, what was he to us? An itch, a fleck, a nothing. Observe the way his legs are jointed, the flexibility of movement –

MULGRAVE: I think it's died.

KING: What?

MULGRAVE: The flea, Your Majesty, it's stopped moving. I'm most dreadfully sorry, I think it's died.

BARBARA enters holding before her a phial containing a white viscous substance.
ROCHESTER follows her, tucking his shirt into his breeches.

BARBARA: We've brought His Majesty a substance truly worthy of his investigation: the noble seed.

ROCHESTER: The elixir of life. As His Majesty requested.

KING: I knew I could rely on you.

The KING empties the phial beneath his lenses for study.

MULGRAVE: What is that? Is it what I fear it to be?

KING: How did you get it in the phial?

ROCHESTER: It was a struggle but Barbara helped me.

BARBARA: It was my pleasure.

MULGRAVE: (*Prudish.*) Your loyalty to His Majesty knows no bounds.

JANE enters.

KING: Mistress Roberts. Have you come to join us?

JANE: I have some guests with me today. They're dining with Lord Mulgrave this evening.

MULGRAVE: Ah.

KING: Well get rid of them if you can, I've something I want to show you.

JANE: My guests desire to meet you, if that were possible.

KING: And they are...?

JANE: My friend Elizabeth and her guardians, Lord Hawley and Sir John Warre.

KING: A brief audience then.

JANE: Thank you, Your Majesty.

JANE exits.

MULGRAVE: Elizabeth Malet is the heiress I told you of.

KING: Ah yes.

MULGRAVE: You will be pleased to know I have put myself forward as a suitor.

Silence.

ROCHESTER: All this... (*Feigns a yawn.*) experimentation has sapped my strength. I may have to retire to my bed.

KING: (*Pointed.*) Surely you're not bashful of meeting Mulgrave's bride-to-be, are you Wilmot?

ROCHESTER: If His Majesty might excuse me? I have performed him services today that might have failed a lesser man.

KING: In Barbara's hands, I doubt it. But you are excused for now.

ROCHESTER: I thank you.

ROCHESTER fails to exit before ELIZABETH, SIR JOHN and HAWLEY enter with JANE.

ELIZABETH: Escaping from someone?

ROCHESTER: My Lady.

ELIZABETH: What have you all been up to in the King's Laboratory?

ROCHESTER: Nothing much to speak of. Tossing off the odd experiment.

KING: Welcome friends.

ROCHESTER: You will excuse me, I have some matters to attend to.

ROCHESTER slips away.

SIR JOHN & HAWLEY: Your Majesty.

KING: Hawley, is it? I recognise your face from the House of Lords. But I don't believe we've spoken, face to face.

HAWLEY: That is true, Sir. I knew your father a little better before he was…before he was…

KING: Beheaded?

HAWLEY: Well, yes. He was a great man, a king, Sir.

KING: And Sir John?

SIR JOHN: Your Majesty.

KING: Did you receive my letter?

SIR JOHN: I did, Sir, thank you.

KING: And this must be Elizabeth. You are lovelier even than your description.

ELIZABETH: My description rather emphasised my dowry than my looks, Your Majesty.

SIR JOHN: Elizabeth!

KING: A mistake on the part of your guardians then, not to emphasise the greater riches.

JANE: Her greatest asset is her virtue. Is that not right, Elizabeth?

BARBARA: I see you've made acquaintance with the Earl of Rochester?

ELIZABETH: Yes, though he seemed anxious to avoid my company just now.

KING: You find him a refreshing change from the stiffs, fops and dodderers your guardians have been parading before you, no doubt?

MULGRAVE bristles.

SIR JOHN: I hope Your Majesty will not be offended if we choose another of Elizabeth's suitors in preference to Lord Rochester.

MULGRAVE bristles further at the mention of ROCHESTER in this context.

KING: Not at all, Sir John, the decision must be yours.

SIR JOHN: Your Majesty.

KING: A safe journey to your lodgings friends, mademoiselle. It has been a pleasure.

SIR JOHN: It has been a privilege to meet you, Your Majesty.

ELIZABETH, SIR JOHN and HAWLEY curtsy or bow. The KING returns to his microscope.

MULGRAVE: Mistress Malet.

ELIZABETH: Oh Mr Mulgrave, I did not see you there?

MULGRAVE: *Lord* Mulgrave. I am an Earl.

SIR JOHN: I'm looking forward to our dinner this evening My Lord.

HAWLEY: Mulgrave is it?

MULGRAVE: The Earl of Mulgrave, yes it is.

SIR JOHN: Half seven. On the dot.

SIR JOHN ushers ELIZABETH and HAWLEY away. JANE is going with them but the KING stops her.

KING: Jane, stay and admire my new magnifying lenses.

JANE: What is it you are magnifying?

BARBARA looks away and smiles.

KING: Seed.

JANE: (*Looking.*) These don't look like seed. Oh? There are creatures there, wriggling.

KING: Wriggling?

JANE: Squirming.

KING: (*Looking.*) You're right. Wilmot's seed seems to contain parasites.

MULGRAVE: May I see, Your Majesty?

JANE: Wilmot's seed?

MULGRAVE: (*Looking.*) So it does.

KING: How very disturbing.

MULGRAVE: Don't you think we should inform him?

JANE: Inform whom of what?

BARBARA: Don't worry yourself child, you've made an important discovery.

JANE: I have?

KING: Well done Jane.

BARBARA: Perhaps you should donate your brain to science?

JANE: Staring down at those, whatever they are…those wrigglers…has put me in something of a swoon. If you would excuse me, Your Majesty, I think I must go to my bed. I feel quite flushed all of a sudden.

KING: Of course.

JANE exits lightheadedly watched by a captivated KING.

BARBARA: In all honesty, I cannot see her appeal.

MULGRAVE: (*Still staring down the lenses.*) You know, I really do think somebody should tell him.

Scene 9 – Abduction

Street (evening): HAWLEY; SIR JOHN; ELIZABETH; ROCHESTER; HOODED MEN; MULGRAVE
HAWLEY, SIR JOHN and ELIZABETH await their carriage.

HAWLEY: Where's the blasted coach? I told the man to be here!

ELIZABETH: That is quite possibly the most tedious meal I have ever had the misfortune to sit through.

SIR JOHN: You might have made more effort to converse with Lord Mulgrave.

ELIZABETH: He might have made more effort not to be such an obnoxious toad.

SIR JOHN: At least we met the King today. He's very kingly, d'you not think? Like a king's supposed to be. Somehow you don't expect them to be how they're supposed to be. I expected to be disappointed but I was not, not one bit. Very kingly he was, the King. Very like a king.

Three HOODED MEN lurk in the shadows.

HAWLEY: (*To ROCHESTER.*) You there! Have you seen a coach and four in the locality?

One of the hooded men (ROCHESTER) draws his sword and advances quickly on HAWLEY.

ROCHESTER: No, but I have a coach and *six* waiting for the lady this way.

The other two HOODED MEN move in to support ROCHESTER.

HAWLEY: (*ROCHESTER's sword at his throat.*) I'm a Peer of the Realm. And a personal friend of King Charles the Second of England.

ROCHESTER: (*His sword threatening to puncture HAWLEY's skin.*) And what of it?

HAWLEY: I'll give you anything you want.

ROCHESTER: I want the young lady to come with me. I assure you, she won't come to any harm.

HAWLEY: Very well. Elizabeth.

SIR JOHN: No no, this is not possible.

ROCHESTER: What if I were to slit the old man's throat?

SIR JOHN: Still it would not be possible. She's my stepdaughter and my responsibility. Under no circumstances is she to leave my supervision.

ROCHESTER: Come with me Elizabeth.

ELIZABETH: Why should I?

HAWLEY: For God's sake child, the man says he'll slit my neck!

ELIZABETH advances towards ROCHESTER. She's the only one who's recognised him.

ROCHESTER: 'Since first my dazzled eyes were thrown on that bewitching face. Like –'

ELIZABETH: (*Interrupting, daring him.*) And why should I accept protestations of love from a man who wears a hood to hide his face?

SIR JOHN: Don't rile him Elizabeth.

ROCHESTER lets his sword drop from HAWLEY's throat and pulls off his hood.

ROCHESTER: Is this better?

ELIZABETH: I'm undecided.

SIR JOHN: You Sir!

HAWLEY: The fruit thief!

ELIZABETH: No, on reflection, I preferred the hood on.

His anxiety showing now, ROCHESTER grabs ELIZABETH's arm and begins to drag her off.

ROCHESTER: Come with me.

ELIZABETH: Don't treat me like a piece of baggage! Let me go!

SIR JOHN: I cannot allow this, let her alone at once!

SIR JOHN advances on ROCHESTER, ROCHESTER flicks his sword and cuts him. SIR JOHN drops to his knees clasping his wounded arm.

I beg you Sir, I beg of you. She's an innocent girl. Don't do this to her, don't do this to her family. We love her, she's a lovely girl. Please, I beg you.

ROCHESTER: She'll come to no harm, I promise you.

SIR JOHN: What do you intend to do?

ROCHESTER: I've made my intentions perfectly clear. I will marry her.

ELIZABETH: Once more, I am the last person whose opinion is sought on this matter.

ROCHESTER: Come with me.

ELIZABETH: Give me one reason why I should?

MULGRAVE has entered and draws his sword.

MULGRAVE: Rochester!

ROCHESTER: (*To ELIZABETH.*) There is one excellent reason.

ROCHESTER hands ELIZABETH rather roughly over to his HOODED ACCOMPLICES.

Take her.

ELIZABETH: Ow! Get off! Get off me!

MULGRAVE: You've overstepped the mark, My Lord.

ROCHESTER: It's a habit I've got into.

ROCHESTER and MULGRAVE clash swords.

You should try it yourself. It's quite invigorating. The King would like to see us all engaging with life like this, following our passions.
(*To his ACCOMPLICES.*) Take her. Go! We'll meet at you know where.

ELIZABETH: No, I will not. No. Get off!

The HOODED MEN carry ELIZABETH off, kicking and screaming.
ROCHESTER calls after his accomplices as he and MULGRAVE fight.

ROCHESTER: I'll kill you both if you so much as scratch her!
And no shouting or coarse language!

ELIZABETH: (*As she is carried out of view.*) Get off me you fuckers!

SIR JOHN: They're getting away.

HAWLEY: Run the bugger through!

SIR JOHN: Elizabeth!

MULGRAVE: These are extreme lengths to go to Rochester.

ROCHESTER: I don't expect you to understand Mulgrave. You have all the passion of an eviscerated toad!

With that ROCHESTER disarms MULGRAVE.

Oh, it's over. I was enjoying that. We must do it again some other time.

MULGRAVE: We must.

ROCHESTER gloats briefly. But then HAWLEY, who is behind him, smashes a bottle over his head. ROCHESTER slumps to the ground. MULGRAVE is upon him in an instant, stamping the sword out of his wrist and placing a boot on ROCHESTER's head, pressing down.

MULGRAVE: I failed to mention, My Lord, I have disturbing news for you. It concerns your spunk.

ROCHESTER is hauled off to a prison cell.

Scene 10 – Tower

*Prison Cell (morning): ROCHESTER; BARBARA; GAOLER
ROCHESTER sits, dejectedly, in his prison cell. BARBARA is shown in by a GAOLER.
ROCHESTER does not look up.*

BARBARA: So, my dear sweet dashing boy, you are detained at His Majesty's pleasure?

ROCHESTER ignores her.

I was touched to hear of your adventure. Though the damage you've done to your standing at Court, and particularly with the King, must have caused you to regret your passion.

ROCHESTER continues to ignore her.

You'll be pleased to hear they've recovered the heiress.

ROCHESTER looks up. BARBARA smiles sweetly.

A number of the King's Men caught up with your accomplices, quite by chance, at St Albans or thereabouts.

ROCHESTER: Was she hurt?

BARBARA: The damage has been mostly to her reputation.

BARBARA touches ROCHESTER's hair, affectionate, despite her teasing. He flinches, irritated by her.

ROCHESTER: Why've you come?

BARBARA: To rescue you, of course. With my assistance, I'm confident your star will rise again. And rise higher. The King likes you. And, really, he doesn't like many people.

ROCHESTER: Then why has he imprisoned me like a criminal?

BARBARA: Because you are a criminal. And you left him no choice. You made a fool of him. He wrote you a letter of recommendation and, by your actions, you have made his judgement appear faulty.

ROCHESTER: His judgement was faulty. He told me to follow my passions and that's what I did.

BARBARA: You cannot blame His Majesty. He cannot be seen to condone let alone forgive kidnap and assault against peers of the realm.

ROCHESTER: He should think of the consequences of what he says.

BARBARA: And so should you. It's unwise to speak treason in the Tower.

ROCHESTER sulks.

So, you were following your passions?

ROCHESTER: I was.

BARBARA: I found the heiress rather plain and spoilt.

ROCHESTER: Your own striking and *mature* beauty must have dazzled her.

BARBARA: Well, you've botched your chances of winning her or her fortune, somewhat.

ROCHESTER: I don't need to be reminded.

BARBARA: Ah but good news: the Navy has won a splendid victory over the Dutch at Lowestoft. His Majesty's delighted.

ROCHESTER: What exactly are you doing here, Barbara? Does the King require more warm spunk for his experiments?

BARBARA: (*A genuine offer.*) If it would raise your spirits.

ROCHESTER: I'm a spent force.

BARBARA: Not true. You're infamous. And if there's one thing the English love more than watching a bright star fall, it's watching an underdog bite back.

ROCHESTER: What do you want from me, Lady Castlemaine, apart from help unmuddling your metaphors?

BARBARA: I've come to help you, as a friend.

ROCHESTER: And if I don't want your friendship?

BARBARA: I've brought ink and paper. You must write to the King.

ROCHESTER: To tell him what?

BARBARA: That you beseech his pardon.

BARBARA hands ROCHESTER ink, pen and paper.

That inadvertency, ignorance of the law and passion were the occasions of your offence. Write.

ROCHESTER: Why?

BARBARA: His Majesty cannot forgive you openly until suitable penance has been seen to have been done.

BARBARA crouches beside ROCHESTER and slips her hand inside his breeches.

Come, don't sulk. I'll get you started.

ROCHESTER with BARBARA's encouragement, begins to write.

BARBARA: Write.

ROCHESTER: 'Inadvertency (*Moans.*)…ignorance of the law…passion…' Will this be enough?

BARBARA: Add some embellishment of your own.

ROCHESTER: That, had I reflected on the consequences of incurring his displeasure, I'd have chose death ten thousand times than done it.

BARBARA: Write it down.

ROCHESTER: That I, in all humility and sense of my fault, cast myself at Your Majesty's feet, beseeching you to pardon my first error, and not suffering this one offence to be my ruin.

BARBARA: Very good.

BARBARA removes her hand and stands.

ROCHESTER: Why have you stopped? I was getting into my flow.

BARBARA: You should write something more.

ROCHESTER: What?

BARBARA: That, to show the sincerity of your contrition, you'll do something for him, for the Crown and for the Country.

ROCHESTER: And what's that?

BARBARA: That you'll go fight the Dutch.

Scene 11 – Position

Palace Interior (afternoon): BURNET; KING; QUEEN; SIR JOHN; ELIZABETH

BURNET: It is being suggested that the plague is divine retribution for the debaucheries of the Court.

KING: Ah.

BURNET: That God is trying to tell us something.

KING: Mmm.

BURNET: That the comet was a portent and we ignored it.

KING: I did not ignore it. I had its path charted by the finest astronomers in England. You don't believe this nonsense, do you Burnet?

BURNET: Your Majesty, I merely report the things I have heard said.

KING: It's nonsense.

BURNET: The people observe their neighbours dying; it is natural that they seek an explanation.

KING: Then it's up to you priests and physicians to give them a reasonable, rational explanation. Your superstitious speculations get in the way of proper investigation. These irresponsible, ill-informed connections between this disease and the behaviour of my courtiers are unhelpful in the extreme.

BURNET: It would surely do no harm to ask certain of your friends to moderate their behaviour, to provide a more wholesome example to the commonality.

KING: And then the city will be cured?

BURNET: Perhaps.

KING: Do you seriously believe that?

BURNET: Do you seriously not believe that unrepentant sinners will be damned?

KING: I believe, for what it's worth, that God will never damn a man for allowing himself a little pleasure.

BURNET: The mind must learn to take delight in virtue.

SIR JOHN and ELIZABETH enter.

KING: Thank you Dr Burnet. It is always interesting to hear your opinions. Sir John.

SIR JOHN: You sent for us, Your Majesty.

BURNET: Your Majesty.

BURNET bows to the KING and exits.

KING: Yes, Sir John. I'm concerned to know how your stepdaughter's marriage arrangements are progressing.

SIR JOHN: (*Struggling.*) We still have a degree of…there are interested parties…

KING: Would you object, Sir John, if I were to speak with Elizabeth alone for a moment?

SIR JOHN: (*The words in brackets are implied not spoken.*) Ah, no, if that will be…(alright with you Elizabeth), I'll… (wait outside).

KING: If you would be so kind. I'll only be a moment.

SIR JOHN: Of course. I'll be just here Elizabeth. Her nerves are…

KING: I'll be gentle with her.

SIR JOHN: Thank you. Yes, I'll…

SIR JOHN exits. The KING smiles at ELIZABETH.

KING: I've formed an impression of you, Elizabeth, as one who speaks her mind. Would that be fair to say?

ELIZABETH: I agree, I speak my mind, as most do, when it suits me.

KING: No, I think you'll find it's a trait much in decline. Style and presentation are felt more appropriate than honesty, it seems, in everyday affairs. You're in an admirable minority, Elizabeth. So will you tell me, truly, of your marriage plans as they now stand?

ELIZABETH: Interest has waned somewhat. My market value is not now perceived as highly as it was.

KING: An unfair question mark hangs over your virtue as a result of the brief time you spend with Lord Rochester's accomplices in St Albans.

ELIZABETH: Most unfair. I was held against my will. My virtue was never threatened.

KING: Your virtue is of little concern to me, I assure you. Only your happiness. You were telling me of your suitors.

ELIZABETH: Sir William Fanshawe withdrew his suit this morning. His family decided the financial demands made by my guardians were too high, considering my situation. That leaves only Lord Mulgrave.

KING: And how are you in yourself, following your ordeal?

ELIZABETH: As well as can be expected.

KING: I confess, I feel in part responsible.

ELIZABETH: There's no reason for His Majesty to feel responsible for the behaviour of his courtiers.

KING: No, I have this on my conscience. I suggested to Lord Rochester personally that he make his advances to you. I encouraged him. However, he took things further than I ever imagined or intended he should do. I would like, in some way, to make amends.

ELIZABETH: His Majesty has already proved kind enough in consigning the obnoxious Lord first to the Tower and, more recently, to the North Sea.

KING: He has been engaged in some heavy fighting of late, off the coast of Norway.

ELIZABETH: You have reports of him?

KING: He has acquitted himself well, heroically in at least one instance. Are you concerned for his safety?

ELIZABETH: No.

KING: I will assume that once again you are speaking your mind.

ELIZABETH: I have no concern for him at all.

KING: I believe you.

ELIZABETH: Good.

KING: Good. I have an offer, an opportunity I would like to push your way. There is a place for you at Court, should you desire. As Lady-in-Waiting on the Queen or any number of suitable positions.

ELIZABETH: A position?

KING: It would mean I would honour and respect you as a friend and occasional bedfellow, were you to agree.

ELIZABETH: You're offering me a position as your mistress?

KING: Speaking plainly: yes.

ELIZABETH: But what of Lady Castlemaine? And, of course, your wife the Queen?

KING: I'll continue to provide for Barbara, as I have always done. She is a valued companion. But age, I find, is hardening her. The Queen, as I'm sure you are aware, has never been an obstacle.

ELIZABETH: I'm uncertain as to whether this is a kind or most insulting offer.

KING: You're under no pressure or obligation to accept. Don't give me your answer now. See how your wedding plans proceed and regard this offer as a contingency. Until then, feel free to come and go as you please. I did not intend adding insult to your injury.

ELIZABETH: No. No, I thank you.

KING: You appear distracted.

ELIZABETH: How many have been killed in this war with the Dutch?

Scene 12 – Fire

Ship at sea (night) into burnt out London street (morning): ANNE; ROCHESTER; BURNET
On a fighting ship in the middle of the North Sea, cannon fire rips through rigging setting it aflame.
On the burning deck, amid smoke and the almost deafening noise of further cannon fire, a man screams in agony. Another man (quite possibly ROCHESTER) cries out desperately for assistance.
Burning timbers crash to the ground. Immense flames crackle and lick at the sky.
There are cries for help, shouts of instruction from rescuers and vain attempts to put out the fire with pails of water.
ROCHESTER steps out from the chaos on to a burnt out London street.

ROCHESTER: Did the fire reach the Palace?

ANNE: No. They pulled down houses in its path to stop its spread.

BURNET: I'm told even the King joined in. Took his coat off.

ANNE: And with buckets of water.

ROCHESTER: God bless him. God bless His Majesty.

ANNE: Come back with me to Spelsbury? Recover from your injuries.

ROCHESTER: My injuries are nothing, mother, to those suffered by many of my fellow soldiers. And for what?

ANNE: Don't go back to the Court. You know now what it is like.

ROCHESTER: I've unfinished business to attend to there.

BURNET: It has certain attractions, I can understand, to a young man such as yourself.

ANNE: He's like his father: you love the Lord your King more than the Lord your God.

ROCHESTER: No.

ANNE: Yes.

ROCHESTER: I'm not returning for love of His Majesty. I'm no longer dazzled by a man who can wage such a useless war for so little reward, save the distraction of his people from the vacuity of his existence.

BURNET: Now even I would not venture such an extreme position.

ANNE: I'm relieved and grateful to the Lord that you're back safe from fighting. But here in London is the greater danger. Where not merely your life but your soul is in peril.

ROCHESTER: Mother. I promise you I will say my prayers.

ROCHESTER goes.

Scene 13 – Blind man's buff

Privy Gardens (afternoon): KING; QUEEN; MULGRAVE; FANSHAWE; BARBARA; ELIZABETH; ROCHESTER

A game of blind man's buff in progress. ELIZABETH, BARBARA, MULGRAVE, FANSHAWE and others play. MULGRAVE is blindfolded. The KING stands apart looking at architectural plans. The QUEEN looks over his shoulder.

MULGRAVE: Where have you got to?

BARBARA: Over here, My Lord.

FANSHAWE: Over here.

MULGRAVE: (*Lunging at someone and missing.*) Damn!

FANSHAWE: And here.

MULGRAVE: Never fear Fanshawe, I have no intention of catching you.

BARBARA: You're not quick enough.

QUEEN: Are they good maps?

KING: Plans.

QUEEN: Plans. You will make London nice?

KING: (*Irritated.*) Yes, yes.

QUEEN: (*Pointing at something on the plans.*) What is this?

KING: The River Thames. See, it has waves. And little boats.

QUEEN: Why you like this to me?

KING: What is the matter now?

QUEEN: We don't try for the baby.

KING: We will try for a baby soon, tomorrow.

MULGRAVE catches ELIZABETH and feels for her features lecherously.

MULGRAVE: Got one! A soft one and it's…

ELIZABETH: (*Pre-empting him and pulling herself free.*) It's me, Elizabeth.

MULGRAVE: (*Removes his blindfold.*) So it is.

ELIZABETH: My turn.

ELIZABETH snatches the blindfold from MULGRAVE and goes to BARBARA who helps her put it on.

KING: Why don't you join in the game?

QUEEN: I don't want to play these stupid game. I don't want to look for stupid boat! I want to fuck for the baby!

The game stops. Silence. All eyes are on the KING and QUEEN. Then the QUEEN turns and exits angrily through the middle of the game. Another uncomfortable pause.

KING: The game! Play the game!

BARBARA: Ready? (*Spins Elizabeth.*) Once for a husband. Twice for a girl. Thrice for a boy child. Another for the world.

MULGRAVE: The world is spinning on its axis.

BARBARA: Once again for love. Twice again for pleasure. Thrice again out of necessity. And another for good measure. Come and catch us!

FANSHAWE: You're cold but getting warmer.

MULGRAVE: Warm, you're getting warm. No cold, colder, over here!

BARBARA: (*Dragging MULGRAVE out of ELIZABETH's path.*) You mustn't try so hard to get caught, My Lord. It's not in the spirit of the game.

FANSHAWE: Over here Elizabeth.

ELIZABETH: I'm getting dizzy.

BARBARA: Come on Elizabeth, you're terrible at this game.

ELIZABETH: (*Laughing.*) I'm trying!

ROCHESTER enters and is accidentally caught up in the game. Surprised to see him, the others stop playing and there is silence. Only ELIZABETH, because she is blindfolded, continues moving, playing the game.

ELIZABETH: Why've you gone silent? Is this a trick? Have you all deserted me?

ROCHESTER stands in the middle of the playing areas, where it is only a matter of time before ELIZABETH 'catches' him.

ELIZABETH: Is anyone there? Who's there? Got you! (*Her hands move to his face.*) And you are…

ROCHESTER delicately removes ELIZABETH's blindfold. She stares up into his face and passes out in his arms.

MULGRAVE: Elizabeth!

BARBARA and MULGRAVE rush to ELIZABETH's assistance. They take her from ROCHESTER and she begins to come round. FANSHAWE produces a glass of wine, which she receives gratefully.

MULGRAVE: Today was the first I saw her laugh and smile in months. Now *you* have returned.

ROCHESTER: I did not expect to find her here.

MULGRAVE: Get away, she does not require your assistance.

ROCHESTER: With so many dead from plague and London sludge and rubble, I didn't expect to find the Court engaged in children's games.

BARBARA: And you criticised us before for not knowing how to enjoy ourselves.

KING: Plague's burnt out Wilmot. And I have plans for London. The fire was a blessing. Out of the ashes we shall rebuild spectacularly in brick and stone. A new beginning. In which you must play your part.

FANSHAWE: We received regular reports of your heroics against the Dutch.

BARBARA: You'll find no man in England has a better reputation for courage.

KING: True, you have redeemed yourself entirely. The business with Mistress Malet is quite forgotten.

ROCHESTER: I'm not certain Mistress Malet has forgotten.

MULGRAVE: You keep away from her!

ROCHESTER: Mulgrave, still defending the lady's honour? I trust your swordsmanship has improved?

MULGRAVE: More so than your manners.

ROCHESTER: You should enlist for the King's Navy. You could learn to fire cannon; it might prove more accurate than your cut and thrust.

MULGRAVE: I have enlisted. It's not my fault the Dutch cowards run away whenever I show up to fight them.

ROCHESTER: All men would be cowards if they dared.

MULGRAVE: What are you suggesting? That I am a coward?

ROCHESTER: No, precisely the opposite.

KING: Wilmot, you have put one lady in a swoon and this gentleman in a bluster, both within two minutes of arriving. My friend, you have been sorely missed.

In a rare display of open affection, the KING embraces ROCHESTER.

MULGRAVE: Why does His Majesty embrace this upstart Lord?

BARBARA: He's back from the dead.

MULGRAVE: What?

BARBARA: You forget your scripture. A father loves his prodigal son more than his loyal son.

ROCHESTER: Your Majesty, might I with your permission speak with Mistress Malet? Since the unfortunate business, I've not had occasion to apologise.

KING: When you've done so, you must allow me to show you my vision of London.

ROCHESTER: Your Majesty.

The KING returns to the scrutiny of his plans. ROCHESTER approaches ELIZABETH.

ROCHESTER: My Lady.

ELIZABETH: My Lord.

The Court dissipates, leaving ROCHESTER and ELIZABETH alone.

ELIZABETH: You must think me contemptible, swooning like that.

ROCHESTER: I'm flattered.

ELIZABETH: You shouldn't be. I'd have thumped you if I'd had the strength. I was already dizzy from the game.

ROCHESTER: I must ask your forgiveness for the wrong I've done you. I behaved impulsively. Insensitively.

ELIZABETH: Foolishly.

ROCHESTER: Wickedly. And I do repent most sincerely.

ELIZABETH: I'm sure you do.

ROCHESTER: It was done for love.

ELIZABETH: Of course. 'Since first your dazzled eyes were thrown…'

ROCHESTER: 'on that bewitching face.'

ELIZABETH: Etcetera.

ROCHESTER: Etcetera.

ELIZABETH: Such a sweet little poem.

ROCHESTER: It was written in a rush.

ELIZABETH: After battling the Dutch and facing death, you must find us all extremely frivolous.

ROCHESTER: An unnecessary tussle over disputed herring fisheries in the North Sea is frivolous in comparison with you. I thought about you often.

ELIZABETH: And I thought of you.

ROCHESTER: You are not yet married?

ELIZABETH: No.

ROCHESTER: Nor engaged, nor promised?

ELIZABETH: My reputation has not recovered from the two nights I spent in St Albans with your associates.

ROCHESTER: Lord Mulgrave remains most intent on your protection.

ELIZABETH: He is very…

ROCHESTER: Persistent?

ELIZABETH: Gallant. (*Beat.*) I need the air. Would you walk with me in the gardens?

ROCHESTER: They'll think I've abducted you a second time.

ELIZABETH: Have you not?

ELIZABETH takes ROCHESTER's arm.

Scene 14 – Wedding

Privy Gardens (evening): ROCHESTER; ELIZABETH; BARBARA; JANE; SIR JOHN; MULGRAVE; HAWLEY; KING
A wedding party gathers around ELIZABETH and ROCHESTER and the happy couple are showered with rice and flowers.
MULGRAVE, SIR JOHN and HAWLEY huddle on the periphery.

SIR JOHN: My Lord, you were Hawley's and my own preferred choice of husband for Elizabeth, if it is of any comfort to you.

MULGRAVE: It is not.

HAWLEY: To watch the family fortune snatched away by a fruit-filching son of an idiot is almost more than the heart can bear.

BARBARA produces two glasses of red wine for the couple, which they drain enthusiastically as the toasts are exclaimed

BARBARA: To my Lord and Lady Rochester!

JANE: To my Lord Highwayman and Lady Riches!

BARBARA: To bed with them!

ROCHESTER and ELIZABETH are lifted up on the shoulders of the wedding guests and are heading from the exit when they are intercepted by the KING.

KING: Congratulations. A perfect match – if I do say so myself. Continue please, I didn't mean to impede your progress.

But ROCHESTER has descended from on high, sensing correctly that the KING wishes a word with him.

BARBARA: We'll go on ahead and prepare her for you My Lord.

ELIZABETH is whisked away with whoops and laughter, leaving the KING and ROCHESTER alone.

KING: So, you have your heiress. And the experiment may continue.

ROCHESTER: I've married her for love not money.

KING: But the money helps, does it not?

ROCHESTER: And I'm off to the country with her.

KING: (*Laughing.*) But you hate the country.

ROCHESTER: Not if she's in it.

KING: Quite. Truth is though, John, we've had a terrible time what with plague and fire and all and, well, we need you here. I need you. (*Beat.*) Clearly, I mustn't delay you any further. Go do your duty.

ROCHESTER: (*Correcting him.*) My pleasure.

KING: Pleasure is your duty. Go.

The KING slaps ROCHESTER's back and, with an air of melancholy, watches him leave.

ROCHESTER breaks into a trot as he approaches the exit.

Interval.

Part Two

Scene 15 – The Country

Bedchamber, Adderbury (morning): ROCHESTER; ELIZABETH; MONTAGU; WYNDHAM; SOLDIERS
ROCHESTER and ELIZABETH sleep.
ROCHESTER talks in his sleep, dreaming MONTAGU and WYNDHAM.

ROCHESTER: I, John Wilmot, swear here, between the sea and sky and by Almighty God, that should I die, I will return to my good friends, Thomas Wyndham and Edward Montagu, and give them notice of the future state that follows death. Edward?

MONTAGU: It has an air of blasphemy.

WYNDHAM: Coward.

MONTAGU: I will die today. I feel it.

ROCHESTER: All I ask is that you come back and tell me what it's like.

MONTAGU: I'm dying here. All you can do is mock me.

ROCHESTER: Thomas, you'll swear with me?

WYNDHAM: I will.

ROCHESTER: Then swear.

WYNDHAM: I, Thomas Wyndham, do swear likewise, by God and by my prick and by everything I live for, that should I die this day, I'll come to you and speak the truth.

ROCHESTER: By your prick!?

WYNDHAM: Believe me, John, I hold it very dear. Wait for me, I'll come to you.

ROCHESTER: Come Edward.

MONTAGU: Very well, I swear. If I die this day…

ROCHESTER: By Almighty God.

MONTAGU: By Almighty God. I'll visit you and speak to you.

ROCHESTER: Join us in our embraces.

MONTAGU: I'll come.

ROCHESTER: My good friends. We are bound together.

ROCHESTER wakes with a start. MONTAGU and WYNDHAM have disappeared.

ELIZABETH: It's your dream again.

ROCHESTER: Montagu and Wyndham were here.

ELIZABETH: You're dreaming.

ROCHESTER: Yes.

ELIZABETH: Tell me what happens.

ROCHESTER: We swear a pact.

ELIZABETH: You and Montagu and Wyndham?

ROCHESTER: Half in jest, half in earnest, and with all due ceremonies of religion, that if any one of us dies that day in battle, he will return and tell the other two all about it.

ELIZABETH: Another of your experiments.

ROCHESTER: It's as it happened the morning of the Battle of Bergen.

ELIZABETH: You've never told me what happened at Bergen?

ROCHESTER: All of us fight, undaunted by Montagu's premonition, till near the end of the action, when Wyndham falls suddenly into such a trembling that he can barely stand. Montagu goes to hold him up and they are there, right there beside me, when the same cannon ball kills Wyndham outright and carries half Montagu's belly away. He dies in my arms, as I lie in your arms now.

ELIZABETH holds ROCHESTER tight.

ROCHESTER: Another pair of meaningless deaths in a meaningless battle in a meaningless war that served nothing, save the King and his whims.

ELIZABETH: Him again.

ROCHESTER: He wants me back in London.

ELIZABETH: I want you here.

ROCHESTER: (*His mood lifting.*) You had me here. Two times last night.

ELIZABETH: Two and a half and I want you here again.

ROCHESTER: Where exactly do you want me?

ELIZABETH: Right here.

ELIZABETH pushes ROCHESTER's head beneath the blankets. He happily obliges and her body enjoys the attentions of his tongue...
...Until several soldiers burst into the room and drag ROCHESTER kicking from the bed.

ELIZABETH: Get your hands... Get your hands off him! How dare you!? How dare you!

SOLDIER 1: My Lady, we are under orders to arrest your husband. But I assure you, we have been instructed not to hurt him.

At which point SOLDIER 2 smashes the butt of his musket down on ROCHESTER's head, rendering him immediately unconscious.
SOLDIER 1 restrains ELIZABETH, while the other SOLDIERS carry ROCHESTER away.

ELIZABETH: No, no. John! Come back with him! Bring him back!

Scene 16 – The mock trial

Palace Interior (day): ROCHESTER; SOLDIER; KING; FANSHAWE; BARBARA; JANE
ROCHESTER, hands tied and a hood over his head, is led into the room and brought to a halt before a mock court, presided over by the KING.

FANSHAWE: (*Impersonating a lawyer.*) The prisoner herepresent is charged on three counts; one: sobriety; two: deserting his royal duty; and three: spending gratuitious amounts of time with his wife in the country.

KING: How does the prisoner plead?

The SOLDIER removes ROCHESTER's hood and his eyes adjust to the light and the grinning faces all around him.

KING: Well, what do you have to say for yourself?

ROCHESTER: (*He cannot resist them.*) Guilty! On all counts, I am guilty!

FANSHAWE: I knew you wouldn't deny it!

ROCHESTER: How am I to be punished?

KING: Bring out the instruments of torture.

BARBARA presents ROCHESTER with wine. And JANE slips herself sexily under ROCHESTER's arm.

You are to serve me here as Minister of Pleasure.

ROCHESTER: With all humility, I submit to this court's authority.

ROCHESTER drains the wine in one.

God, I'm thirsty.

JANE: Moisten your lips on mine.

ROCHESTER hesitates only momentarily before kissing JANE extravagantly to cheering from the assembled courtiers.

KING: Let us experiment once again!

Scene 17 – The country wife

Drawing Room, Adderbury (day): ELIZABETH; ANNE ELIZABETH has just received and read a letter.

ELIZABETH: How dare he!

ANNE: You have news?

ELIZABETH: The King it was who instructed those animals to break in and assault John, and carry him away from me.

ANNE: Is he safe?

ELIZABETH: I've been out of my mind with worry.

ANNE: Is he injured?

ELIZABETH starts to leave.

ANNE: Where are you going?

ELIZABETH: To fetch him back.

ANNE: Do not fight the King for your husband's heart.

ELIZABETH: Why not?

ANNE: You will lose.

ELIZABETH: Like you did with your husband?

ANNE: Yes.

ELIZABETH: What do you propose I do then?

ANNE: Wait.

ELIZABETH: Like you waited for your husband? Until he was dragged back to you a corpse?

ANNE: Your place is here. He would have sent for you if he had wanted you to follow. He will return when he is able. Comfort yourself that he is safe.

ELIZABETH: I wasn't born to wait.

ANNE: Your place is here.

ELIZABETH: And yours?

ANNE: I will remain with you. So long as I am welcome.

ELIZABETH rolls her eyes at this but she has now lost the impetus to leave.

ELIZABETH: At least, as you say, we know he's safe.

Scene 18 – Imperfect enjoyment

Bedchamber (morning): ROCHESTER; JANE
Clothes and empty bottles scattered around two bodies in the bed: ROCHESTER and JANE (unseen under the sheets at the start of the scene).

ROCHESTER: 'Naked she lay, clasped in my longing arms,
    I filled with love, and she all over charms, (*JANE giggles.*)
    Both equally inspired with eager fire,
    Melting through kindness, flaming in desire; (*JANE moans.*)
    With arms, legs, lips, close clinging to embrace,
    She clips me to her breast, and sucks me to her face.
        (*They kiss.*)
    Her nimble tongue (love's lesser lightning) played
    Within my mouth, and to my thoughts conveyed
    Swift orders that I should prepare to throw
    The all-dissolving thunderbolt below. (*JANE enthuses.*)
    My fluttering soul, sprung with a pointed kiss,
    Hangs hovering o'er her balmy brinks of bliss, (*JANE squirms.*)
    But whilst her busy hand would guide that part,
    Which should convey my soul up to her heart,'

JANE: Oh yes!

ROCHESTER: 'In liquid raptures I dissolve all o'er,'

JANE: (*Simulates great frustration.*) Oh no!

ROCHESTER: 'Melt into sperm, and spend at every pore.'

JANE: Such a disappointment.

ROCHESTER: 'A touch from any part of her had done't,
Her hand, her foot, her very look's a cunt.'

JANE: I've had it happen to me, with other men, before last night. But you're the first to have composed a poem in honour of the event.

ROCHESTER: It's happened before, you say?

JANE: And to better men than you.

ROCHESTER: The King?

JANE: Never the King. And considering the not inconsiderable dimensions of the royal prick...

ROCHESTER: Do we have to?

JANE: ...must make it all the more difficult to control.

ROCHESTER: How big is it then?

JANE demonstrates.

ROCHESTER: Is that up or down?

JANE: That's up. Down it's a little smaller.

Jane demonstrates again.

ROCHESTER: Not much though?

JANE: Not that much smaller, no. It's certainly the biggest I've ever...experienced.

ROCHESTER: And you've experienced...?

JANE: Forty eight now, including yours.

ROCHESTER: Up?

JANE: Up of course! Almost always.

ROCHESTER: Forty eight!

JANE: So far.

ROCHESTER: And you were such an irritating virgin. I like you better now.

JANE: I like it better too. Are you more yourself this morning?

ROCHESTER: Perhaps with a glass of wine inside me.

JANE: Before you've even left the bed?

ROCHESTER: I've to be inebriated for the King at noon. It's expected. I have to entertain the Court.

JANE: What's happening at noon?

ROCHESTER: Some appalling new dirge by the Keeper of the King's instruments and then he's unveiling something special in the privy garden.

JANE: Not for the first time.

JANE is up and getting dressed.

ROCHESTER: It's hard work being infamous.

JANE: It's hardly working in the fields.

ROCHESTER: You think I enjoy all this pleasure?

JANE: What else is there to enjoy?

ROCHESTER: Love? Good works? Religion?

JANE: Little wonder you're dissolving into sperm if you're contemplating good works and religion while satisfying me. Or attempting to.

ROCHESTER: Where are you going?

JANE: To fetch your wine.

ROCHESTER: Ring for a servant.

JANE: I have my reputation to think of.

ROCHESTER: Your reputation is as the best fuck in London.

JANE: And so I wouldn't want the servants spreading word that the hardest living gent in Christendom must be drunk to keep it up for me. (*Beat.*) I'm tired of pretending to be your mistress.

ROCHESTER: You call this pretending?

JANE: If the King prefers me to Barbara, then he should tell her.

ROCHESTER: I'm offended you're not content being thought of as my mistress.

JANE: And I'm offended that, drunk or sober, you can't control your wayward gism. Do you have the same difficulty with your wife?

ROCHESTER: Not that I recall. What are you doing?

JANE: Gathering your clothes.

ROCHESTER: Ring for a servant to do it.

JANE: No.

ROCHESTER: Give them to me, I want to dress.

JANE: I think Elizabeth is your problem. I hope you're not so unfashionable as to be enamoured of and pining for your own wife, My Lord. If word got around that you were, your reputation would suffer greatly.

ROCHESTER: Give me my clothes.

JANE: They need an airing.

ROCHESTER: Give them here!

JANE: Come and get them, if you dare!

Scene 19 – Exposure

Privy Garden (day): MULGRAVE; BARBARA; ROCHESTER; JANE
MULGRAVE and BARBARA walk in the garden.

MULGRAVE: He is drunk for a majority of the time. He is vulgar, insulting. Case in point: the diplomatic scandal when 'in error I do assure you Monsieur' he passed pornographic verses to the French Ambassador in place of the Declaration of Indulgence?

BARBARA: I doubt the Ambassador was genuinely shocked, from what I know of him. Most filthy verses are, in any case, translations from the French.

MULGRAVE: You know he's established what he calls a 'Committee for the Expungement of Bad Poetry'. He ridiculed in public the Poet Laureate's newest work and, what is more, had him physically assaulted in Covent Garden as punishment it is said for being 'tedious'.

BARBARA: Is that true?

MULGRAVE: It is rumoured to be true, yes.

BARBARA: Ah.

MULGRAVE: He's 'declared war' he says 'on tedium in its many and varied forms' and has set about hounding the respectable poets and playwrights of the town.

BARBARA: We can but hope the play that you are writing meets with His Lordship's approval when it is presented.

JANE (carrying Rochester's clothes) appears with ROCHESTER (dressed only in a bedsheet) in pursuit. JANE puts MULGRAVE and BARBARA between her and ROCHESTER.

BARBARA: My Lord, I see you come to us in the Roman style.

JANE: It's the very pinnacle of fashion this year in Paris, I believe.

ROCHESTER: Remarkably, you seem to retain some authority around here Barbara, albeit unmerited. Perhaps you would ask Mistress Roberts to return my clothes.

JANE: I'll return your clothes, My Lord, just as soon as you return my bed linen.

ROCHESTER, brazen, removes his toga and tosses it towards JANE. MULGRAVE is understandably appalled.

MULGRAVE: I can smell your whore on you Rochester.

ROCHESTER: The tragedy is that that's as close as you'll ever come to enjoying yourself Mulgrave.

BARBARA: It's a pity the Queen's not with us. She always enjoys the more visual entertainments.

MULGRAVE: You realise that anyone could see you here…. Women, royalty, visiting officials.

ROCHESTER: One doesn't come to London and to the Court if one doesn't wish to be seen.

JANE reneges on her agreement and exits, laughing with both ROCHESTER's clothes and her bed sheet.

ROCHESTER: Now, if you'll excuse me.

ROCHESTER tears off after JANE.

MULGRAVE: I rest my case.

Scene 20 – Viscera

Council room (background) and laboratory (foreground) (afternoon): COUNCILLORS; KING; ROCHESTER
The King's Secret Executive Committee in session in the background (or offstage). The KING is in the foreground dissecting a toad.

COUNCILLOR 1: I'm merely concerned that so many of the families that were against the Crown during the civil war remain in possession of their lands and property.

COUNCILLOR 2: Antagonising old Parliamentarians will not help us re-establish the monarchy as a national institution accepted by all parties.

COUNCILLOR 1: I think it only just that those who took Cromwell's side against the King should have their lands confiscated.

COUNCILLOR 2: And given to such people as you?

COUNCILLOR 1: And given to such people as fought for His Majesty.

COUNCILLOR 2: You forget that His Majesty's Act of Indemnity and Oblivion means…

COUNCILLOR 1: Indemnity for his enemies and oblivion for his friends.

COUNCILLOR 3: The difficulty is the crown has been stripped of its tax-raising powers. His Majesty can achieve nothing without money. The reason we had to negotiate a peace with the Dutch was because Parliament refused to give him anything approaching enough money to fight a decent war.

COUNCILLOR 2: Which returns us to the main business of the day: that Parliament has requested the account books, in order to trace what it calls 'the actual use' made of money voted for the war with Holland.

COUNCILLOR 1: 'The actual use'! 'The actual use'! Do they call His Majesty a thief? Is this to be tolerated?

ROCHESTER joins the KING.

KING: It took me so long to get here. Years of war, on the run, in exile.

ROCHESTER: You were always King. It merely took the people a while to realise it.

KING: So much was expected of me at my Restoration.

ROCHESTER: And is still.

KING: Now I'm here, I find myself longing for the days of excitement and danger. After Worcester, with your father, on the run, risking life and limb, fighting for the realm. / Sheltered...

ROCHESTER: Mostly unsuccessfully.

KING: ...by the real people of England.

ROCHESTER: And their wives.

KING: And their daughters.

ROCHESTER: And that bastard oak tree.

KING: All risking their lives for me. Sharing a crust of bread with me at their tables with the shutters shut, talking in whispers after sundown.

ROCHESTER: The English affection for the underdog.

KING: I've never felt the same from people since. Even the day I returned, travelling through Kent, arriving in London to the cheers. It wasn't the same.

ROCHESTER: It's not just about you.

KING: What?

ROCHESTER: The Restoration. It's not just about you.

KING: I feel the weight of everyone's expectations. Really, I do. But I'm powerless. Parliament won't give me the money to do anything. Look at our half-baked war with the Dutch.

ROCHESTER: I lost friends in that half-baked war.

KING: It distracted people from their miserable situation at home for a little while, nothing more.

ROCHESTER: One screamed for an hour, bleeding to death in my arms.

KING: Oh bloody hell John, get over it.

ROCHESTER: Don't you think you should be doing something other than indulging your curiosity, servicing your senses, shagging, poking at the viscera of toads? Shouldn't you be doing good?

KING: What good is there to be done? Show me John. Show me something good and I'll do it. (*Beat.*) I'm encouraging science.

ROCHESTER: Science!

KING: Knowledge that can be used for good.

ROCHESTER: You pretend to be seeking knowledge, when all you truly seek is distraction.

KING: We've reduced God to a rumour. Politics to a scuffle in the dust for the loose change. Knowledge is all that remains.

ROCHESTER: You can be fucking melancholy sometimes Your Majesty, if you don't mind me saying.

KING: We need some new experiments.

ROCHESTER does an exaggeratedly pompous impression of BURNET.

ROCHESTER: (*BURNET voice.*) Might I ask what space there is in your experiments in life and in your instruments of pleasure for the words and ways of God?

KING: (*Playing the game.*) My scientific instruments are instruments of worship with which I may observe the details of God's creation, Mr Burnet. God's truth is in the details.

ROCHESTER: (*BURNET voice.*) It is Popery that thrills in instruments, frippery, icons, golden calves of so-called 'worship'. It is in our hearts that we should hope to find God, not in the cogs and wheels of man-made machinery.

KING: Is Mankind not the greatest of God's creations? Are not Mankind's achievements God's?

ROCHESTER: (*BURNET voice.*) It is a mistake to put Mankind's achievements on the same scale as God's. Enlightenment is not in the products of Creation, but in the reasons for it.

KING: Are you going to satirise Burnet's opinions or merely regurgitate them?

ROCHESTER: (*He's dropped the voice.*) I don't know anything that infuriates you more than Burnet's opinions.

KING: You derive pleasure from infuriating me?

ROCHESTER: I agree with Burnet that something is lost when you reduce it to its constituent parts. Look at that toad. You take a thing apart but you can't put it back together. When you're done, you cast aside the useless pieces. When all possible scientific questions have been answered the problems of life remain untouched.

KING: Don't abandon me John. I need you with me. You understand / the experimental life.

ROCHESTER: I want to spend more time in the country with Elizabeth.

KING: ... Challenging expectations. Exploring where there is no light.

ROCHESTER: I married her for love, I told you that.

KING: You married her for love of me. So you could be with me. Your duty is to be with me. We're in a rut John. Nothing more. It's down to you to get us out.

The COUNCIL need the KING.

COUNCILLOR 2: Your Majesty?

KING: Gentlemen, let us reconvene tomorrow.

COUNCILLOR 1: Your Majesty, this question of the accounts – ?

KING: Can't we forget the frigging accounts for just a few hours!

COUNCILLOR 3: Your Majesty?

KING: Take me somewhere.

ROCHESTER: Some low amusement?

KING: Some low amusement, yes.

Scene 21 – Low amusement

Brothel (evening): KING; ROCHESTER; MRS TASKER; PROSTITUTES; SERVANT
Dumbshow: ROCHESTER helps the KING don a disguise (basically a dressing down). They approach MRS TASKER and exchange pleasantries. She brings them wine. They do a deal with her. MRS TASKER leads the KING behind a screen, where PROSTITUTES undress him. ROCHESTER asks MRS TASKER for more wine, indicating that the KING will pay. MRS TASKER brings him wine and exits. As the KING's clothes are hung over the screens, ROCHESTER bides his time, drinks and listens.

PROSTITUTE 1: (*Off.*) Giddy-up there! Can't you go no faster!

PROSTITUTE 2: (*Off.*) S'there room up there for another?

KING: (*Off.*) Yes!

PROSTITUTE 1: (*Off.*) Yes!

PROSTITUTE 2: (*Off.*) Yes!

KING & PROSTITUTES 1 & 2: (*Off.*) Yes!

KING: (*Off.*) The winner!

*ROCHESTER gathers the KING's clothes, checks they contain
the KING's moneybag and exits.*

KING: (*Off.*) Mrs Tasker!
(*Appears, postcoital, wearing only a shirt.*) Mrs Tasker!

MRS TASKER: (*Entering.*) Finished already Sir?

KING: Mrs Tasker, where are my clothes?

MRS TASKER: I couldn't tell you Sir.

KING: Someone has taken my clothes.

MRS TASKER: Weren't no-one in my employ, Sir, I run a
respectable business.

KING: Where's the gentleman with whom I arrived?

MRS TASKER: I left him here, Sir. It must have been him
what took off with your clothes hisself, as a form of
gentleman humour.

KING: You understand I cannot pay you till my clothes are
returned? For no better reason than my money is in the
pockets.

MRS TASKER: Oh I understand Mister, I hear this story
regular. You Court gentlemen is easily free with your
own money when you got it, but when you've not, you'd
as easy make free with other people's. And you'll spout
all manner of incredulous tales of how it is at this
particular moment you's incapable of paying for goods
and services what you've received in full knowing of
your skint condition.

KING: Mrs Tasker –

MRS TASKER: I know, I know, you'll be telling me you're
a gentleman and your credit's as good as your word and
you're an honest fellow and likely a confidant of the
King hisself. I've heard all your tales and excuses, and
from finer mouths than grace your ugly mug. It's all a
lark to you innit? But I'm telling you, some of us can't

afford to let gents such as yourself leave without paying for the price of a lark. Ain't funny to us, you see. My husband's upstairs, I warn you, he's big and don't appreciate the finer points of the gentlemanly humours.

KING: Here, take my ring as security. Fetch me a set of clothes. I'll be on my way and will send payment immediately I get home.

MRS TASKER: What's this?!

KING: It's a ring. I'm offering it to you as security. It's worth several thousand times my debt to you. Now fetch me a set of clothes.

MRS TASKER: (*Scoffing.*) Look at these stones!

KING: I can assure you that is as valuable a piece of jewellery as you / will ever see.

MRS TASKER: You ain't asking me to believe these is real?

KING: God damn you Wilmot.
If you look carefully, you will notice upon the ring the Royal Stuart coat of arms

MRS TASKER: Which proves what?

KING: Which proves, you stupid fucking tart, that I –

A SERVANT has entered with a package.

MRS TASKER: What do you want?

SERVANT: A gentleman outside has asked me to deliver this package and this note to another gentleman: this gentleman here, if I'm not mistaken, as the other gentleman told me I would find him in receipt of your hospitality and wearing very little in the way of clothing.

Here you are Sir, I'm to deliver this package and read you – and I can read thank you very much, being better educated than my station would imply – this note. Your face seems not unfamiliar to me, Sir, if you don't mind my saying so.

(*Spots the ring in MRS TASKER's hand*) What's that?

MRS TASKER: It's the gentleman's ring.

The SERVANT looks at the KING, the ring, and the KING again. Then drops to his knees.

What are you doing now?

KING: Give me the package.

The KING takes the package: it is his clothes. He dresses.

Haven't you forgotten something?

SERVANT: (*Remembers the note.*) Yes. My humble apologies, Your... It is in the form of a poem, Your –

KING: Read it.

SERVANT: I obey –

KING: Read!

SERVANT: 'In the Isle of Britain long since famous grown For breeding the best...'

KING: Read!

SERVANT: '...cunts in all Christendom'

MRS TASKER: Did he say 'cunts'?

SERVANT: I confess, I did Madam.

'There now does live, and oh, long may he reign and thrive
The easiest king and the best bred man alive...'

– That's very pertinent and true that; I endorse that sentiment.

'Peace is his aim, his gentleness is such,
And love he loves, for he loves fucking much.
Nor are his high desires above his strength
His sceptre and his prick are of an equal length...'

– It's quite complimentary in its way, ain't it, but this next bit –

KING: I did not ask you for a critique, just read the poem.

SERVANT: 'Restless he rolls about from whore to whore…'

– Oops no, I missed a bit –

The KING, now dressed, snatches the poem and exits.

MRS TASKER: Here wait, you haven't paid!

SERVANT: I'd leave it Mrs Tasker, if I were you.

MRS TASKER: Why, what do you know?

SERVANT: Didn't you recognise his royal presence?

MRS TASKER: I will when I see him again.

SERVANT: That was Good King Charles himself, the King.

MRS TASKER: Oh dear Lord!

SERVANT: Are they of a length, then, his sceptre and his…?

Scene 22 – Smell of the country/stink of the town

Drawing Room, Adderbury (afternoon): ELIZABETH; ROCHESTER; ANNE
A gentle rustic scene: ELIZABETH embroiders. She does not see ROCHESTER enter and put down his bags. He throws his arms around her from behind. Instinctively, she stabs his hand with her needle and they spring apart.

ROCHESTER: Ow!

ELIZABETH impersonates MULGRAVE, flourishing her needle like a sword:

ELIZABETH: 'You have overstepped the mark, My Lord.'

ROCHESTER: 'You should try it some time. It's quite invigorating.' Ow.

ELIZABETH lunges at ROCHESTER. He disarms and overpowers her.

ROCHESTER: You smell of the country.

ELIZABETH: You stink of the town.

They kiss.

You're bleeding. Let me kiss your hand?
To what do I owe the unexpected pleasure of your company?

ROCHESTER: Do I need reason to visit my own wife?

ELIZABETH: Are you out of favour with His Majesty?

ROCHESTER: Leave my hand and kiss my face again.

ELIZABETH: Don't imagine you can abandon me in the country for months and months and then collect your forsaken kisses all at once. Kisses are not your right, they must be earned.

ROCHESTER: Did you not receive my letters?

ELIZABETH: Did you not receive my portrait?

ROCHESTER: Dear God, your portrait. It put me in a great fright lest it be like you. By the size of the head, I thought you must be far gone in the rickets.

ELIZABETH: I thought it a good likeness.

ROCHESTER: I'm relieved to see you now restored to your natural proportions. Kiss me now, I'll give as many kisses as I receive. It's a fair exchange.

ELIZABETH: You think me vain?

ROCHESTER: No.

ELIZABETH: You think I had my portrait painted out of vanity?

ROCHESTER: No.

ELIZABETH: The truth is, husband, I had it painted out of boredom. I thought it would enliven married life a touch to stand motionless for a week, staring sweetly at the backside of an easel.

ROCHESTER: I've stayed away too long.

ELIZABETH: I've been going out of my mind with music and embroidery!
(*Notices ROCHESTER is not listening to her.*) Why are you smiling?

ROCHESTER: I've been working on a satire of the Court.

ELIZABETH: To your own great amusement I see?

ROCHESTER: You've given me my next line.

ROCHESTER starts to rummage in his bags for his papers.

ELIZABETH: A few moments with me and, already, you are thinking of the Court.

ROCHESTER: Let me show it you.

ELIZABETH: Would you like to see my embroidery?

ROCHESTER: Yes.

ELIZABETH: Of course you would not.

ROCHESTER: I would like to see it.

ELIZABETH: I've written some poetry myself. Would you like to see that?

ROCHESTER: Yes.

ELIZABETH: No you wouldn't.

ROCHESTER: Yes I would.

ELIZABETH: I would like to see my husband.

ROCHESTER: You can't expect me to stay here always, living off your money.

ELIZABETH: No, you must go to London to spend it, / leaving me…

ROCHESTER: I'm in the service of the King.

ELIZABETH: …amongst your relations. Which is the worst of all damnations.

ROCHESTER: What do you mean 'amongst my relations'?

ELIZABETH: Your mother is still here.

ANNE: John.

ROCHESTER: Why have you remained so long at Adderbury, Mother?

ELIZABETH: To better criticise my domestic arrangements.

ANNE: I've made one or two suggestions that I hoped would be of use. Mr Burnet tells me…

ROCHESTER: You should not believe everything Burnet says.

ANNE: I've not yet told you what he said.

ROCHESTER: You know the jugglings of priests. They'll twist any event or saying to their own purpose. Which is to show how steeped we are in sin, how close to hand is damnation, and how much we are in need of priests to save us.

ANNE: You speak like a court wit.

ROCHESTER: I am a court wit.

ANNE: I've heard you called the King's Pimp.

ROCHESTER: 'King's Pimp' has a certain ring.

ANNE: You're dazzled by him.

ROCHESTER: Mother…

ANNE: You're dazzled by his celebrity. The King of all England. You're like your father.

ROCHESTER: I'm celebrated too you know.

ANNE: But for what?

ROCHESTER: My wit.

ELIZABETH: At Court, 'wits are treated like common whores. First enjoyed, then kicked out of doors.'

ROCHESTER: You've been reading my poems.

ELIZABETH: They're circulated widely. We get them even in darkest Oxfordshire.

ROCHESTER: I'm more celebrated than I thought.

ELIZABETH: Have you been 'kicked out of doors'?

ROCHESTER: Only temporarily.

ELIZABETH: You come to me when you've nowhere else to go.

ROCHESTER: This is not the welcome I'd hoped for.

ELIZABETH: Say something witty then, for us. We deserve that, at least.

ROCHESTER: It's been a long journey. I'm tired and in need of a drink.

ELIZABETH: How long do you intend to stay?

ROCHESTER: I must return to London within the week.

ELIZABETH: It seems the King, who brought us together, now determines to keep us apart.

ROCHESTER: A week is a long time in the Country.

ELIZABETH: I think you only wanted me for my money so you could be with him.

ROCHESTER: You got a title.

ELIZABETH: I wanted you.

ROCHESTER: Mulgrave has a play opening next week.

ELIZABETH: (*Sarcastic.*) Well, you mustn't miss that.

ROCHESTER: It will be desperately amusing.

ELIZABETH: I could come with you to London.

> ROCHESTER *does not respond to this suggestion with the enthusiasm for which ELIZABETH had hoped.*

ELIZABETH: You don't think much of this proposition?

ROCHESTER: No, I –

ELIZABETH: I expected that your affection for me might not last so very long. Though, by marrying you, I did hope at least for some excitement. But it seems I'm destined to dwindle into a wife sooner than I'd anticipated. (*Beat.*) I expect you've been whoring in London? Or have a mistress?

ROCHESTER: Come with me to London.

ELIZABETH: It was a foolish suggestion. Wives are humiliated for sport in London, I know it. Stay with me for a week. Give me all your attention. Shower me with your kisses. Then go. Watch this play but come back quickly afterward to tell me everything about it.

ROCHESTER: Every painful detail. Every dismal rhyme, every missed dramatic opportunity.

ELIZABETH: And don't think of Mulgrave while making love to me.

> ANNE *huffs and puffs as* ROCHESTER *and* ELIZABETH *canoodle.*

Scene 23 – Mock-King

Theatre: Auditorium, stage and back-stage (afternoon): NELL; TOM; KING; BARBARA; MULGRAVE; FANSHAWE; ROCHESTER

Actors NELL and TOM are backstage, watching as the KING and BARBARA take their seats in the auditorium for Mulgrave's play.

TOM: There's His Majesty arriving.

NELL: Did you hear about his going up Mrs Tasker's?

TOM: I heard it but I don't believe it. Him in a place like that, when he's got a dozen perfumed mistresses up at the Palace. It don't make sense.

NELL: I spoke to the girl what done him. She said he wanted her to ride him like a horse!

TOM: He never did!

NELL: That's what she said. And that he's hung like a Thoroughbred and all. I thought you wasn't in this play.

TOM: Late amendments.

NELL: Not again.

ROCHESTER and FANSHAWE arrive backstage with a horse-head and a prominent set of strap-on genitals.

TOM: Is that my costume?

ROCHESTER: Fanny and I spent all last night making it.

FANSHAWE: I stuffed and he stitched.

An excited MULGRAVE joins the KING and BARBARA in the Royal Box.

MULGRAVE: Your Majesty, we are about to begin. There's a prologue first. Written in your honour.

KING: Excellent.

The play begins. NELL walks on stage, clears her throat and, intent on catching the KING's eye, speaks her prologue directly to him.

NELL: 'In the Isle of Britain long since famous grown
For breeding the best men in Christendom…'

KING: This seems familiar.

BARBARA: Is it not one of Rochester's?

MULGRAVE: No no, this is all my own work, I assure you.

Back-stage ROCHESTER and FANSHAWE complete the dressing of TOM as a Mock-KING.

ROCHESTER: What can you see in this?

TOM: Bugger all.

FANSHAWE: Are you sure this is a good idea?

On-stage…

NELL: 'There reigns, and oh, long may he thrive
The noblest prince and best-bred man alive.
His crown…'

In the Royal Box, MULGRAVE leans across the KING to explain his meaning. The KING is more interested in the actress.

MULGRAVE: Meaning his head, your head. Or brain.

NELL: '…the fount of its refined learning…'

MULGRAVE: An allusion to your scientific achievements.

NELL: 'His sure foot firm, his heart…'

ROCHESTER bursts onto the stage and interrupts NELL. He has papers.

ROCHESTER: '… His stomach churning!'

KING: I wasn't aware you'd written a part for Rochester in your play, Mulgrave.

MULGRAVE is open-jawed.

ROCHESTER: I have some late amendments to make to this play. (*Handing his script to NELL.*) Read this, with the marked changes.

MULGRAVE: Will you get off the stage and allow the actors to continue?!

ROCHESTER: You heard the author Nell: continue.

NELL curtsies and reads falteringly from the new script.

NELL: 'God bless our good and gracious King
Whose promise none relies on.
Who never said a foolish thing
Nor ever did a wise one.'

ROCHESTER has dragged TOM as the Mock-KING onto the stage to be paraded.

ROCHESTER: (*Prostitute voice.*) Giddy-up there! Can't you go no faster!?

MULGRAVE storms on to the stage.

MULGRAVE: This is grossly insulting to His Majesty.

MULGRAVE attempts to shove TOM back into the wings.

ROCHESTER: Your play is an insult to His Majesty: a blunt-fisted attempt to crush the Restoration Spirit.

MULGRAVE: You have allowed my play to progress no further than the first line of the prologue.

ROCHESTER: For which I deserve the enduring gratitude of the theatre-going public.

MULGRAVE: Philistine! You disrupt an important work of literature, a work which has taken months of preparation, in order to parade obscene objects before gentlewomen and, in public, mock no lesser person than your King. Who the devil do you think you are?

ROCHESTER takes the opportunity to squeeze NELL lasciviously.

ROCHESTER: I am Minister of Pleasure and I say your play is shit.

MULGRAVE: What would your wife think of this display were she to see it?

ROCHESTER: Elizabeth loves the theatre. I'm certain she'd approve.

MULGRAVE: You insult her. By cavorting drunkenly and publicly with whores…

NELL: I'm an actress!

MULGRAVE: …you insult your wife and her family. Which, considering that her marrying you in the first instance was the most supreme act of charity –

ROCHESTER: (*Furious.*) A what!?

MULGRAVE: I said Sir, that Elizabeth, your wife, married you as an act of charity.

ROCHESTER: Your meaning, Sir?

MULGRAVE: My meaning, Sir, being that, since you yourself had no estate to speak of –

ROCHESTER thumps MULGRAVE in the face and sends him reeling. He picks himself up.

MULGRAVE: You have drawn blood.

ROCHESTER: Consider it an act of charity.

MULGRAVE: You have assaulted me. That is a crime. And crimes committed in view of the King are punishable, at the very least, by the amputation of the offending hand.

MULGRAVE looks up at the Royal Box but to his great disappointment notes the King is no longer there (he and BARBARA have discreetly slipped away). ROCHESTER, meanwhile has acquired a pair of rapiers from the prop box. He tosses one to MULGRAVE.

ROCHESTER: Let's give these people some genuine entertainment. Are we of a length?

MULGRAVE stares hatefully at ROCHESTER.

ROCHESTER: My Lord are you satisfied our rapiers are of a length?

MULGRAVE: I am satisfied.

ROCHESTER prepares to fight, swishing his foil around extravagantly. Suddenly, he winces with pain.

ROCHESTER: Uh! Fetch me some wine, Fanny. I'm in imminent peril of sobriety.

FANSHAWE: (*Obliging.*) My Lord, for once, I think perhaps you are taking matters a little far.

ROCHESTER: Not at all Fanny. I'm collecting valuable evidence for my latest scientific theory that the more a turd is stirred, the more it stinks.

ROCHESTER drinks from the wine bottle FANSHAWE has provided.

MULGRAVE: Dutch courage Rochester?

ROCHESTER: Dutch courage does not exist. No more so than English decency or Danish wit.

ROCHESTER tosses the empty bottle aside and launches himself at MULGRAVE.
In between furious bouts of fighting, ROCHESTER taunts MULGRAVE with the following poem:

ROCHESTER:
Bursting with pride, the loathed impostune swells,
Prick him, he sheds his venom straight, and smells
But 'tis so crude a scribbler, that he writes,
With as much force to nature as he fights.
And, with his arm and head, his brain's so weak
That his starved fancy is compelled to rake
Among the excrements of others' wit,
To make a stinking meal of what they shit.

In the process of the fight, TOM (unable to see well enough through his horse-head to get out of the way in time) is fatally wounded by ROCHESTER's sword.
The fight stops and everyone gathers around the dying actor.
ROCHESTER removes the horse-head..

TOM: It hurts. This blood is real. It hurts.

FANSHAWE: I think, My Lord, you should seriously consider leaving.

A mortified ROCHESTER takes FANSHAWE's advice.

MULGRAVE: Coward!

Scene 24 – The Queen's children

Court (morning): QUEEN; KING; MULGRAVE; BARBARA; BURNET
The QUEEN passes across the stage searching for her (non-existent) children.

QUEEN: Alfredo! José! Anrique! Alfredo! Alfredo! Onde estão eles? *(Where are they?)*

The KING, BARBARA and MULGRAVE enter.

MULGRAVE: Your Majesty, it is an outrage! He has deliberately and maliciously sabotaged an important cultural event, he has ridiculed Your Majesty to your face, he has caused the death a young thespian of undoubted promise and flown the scene in the most despicably cowardly fashion... Is he to be punished now?

Before the KING can answer, the QUEEN enters, distraught and makes a beeline for BARBARA.

QUEEN: Ondo estão os meus filhos!? *(Where are my children?)*

BARBARA: (?)

QUEEN: Where are my children?

BARBARA: You have no children, Your Royal Highness,

QUEEN: Ondo estão os meus filhos!? *(Where are my children?)* Ela assassinou os meus filhos!? *(She has murdered my children!)*

BARBARA: What's she saying?

QUEEN: She has murdered my children!

BARBARA: For pity's sake –

The QUEEN is restrained by the KING as she attempts to attack BARBARA.

QUEEN: Assasinas! *(Murderess!)*

KING: Catharine.

QUEEN: Assasinas! Assasinas!

KING: Barbara, would you leave us?

BARBARA: No, I won't. Why should I? She's clearly demented.

QUEEN: Eu matá-la-ei! *(I will kill her!)*

KING: Your presence here is causing distress to the Queen.

BARBARA: And when has that ever been a problem?

KING: Don't make me choose between you.

BARBARA: There is no choice to make. The Queen and I fulfil entirely separate functions.

KING: Will you leave?

BARBARA: Are you banishing me?

KING: I'm not banishing you, I'm asking you to leave.

QUEEN: Assasinas! / Assasinas! Assasinas! Assasinas!

BARBARA: You'll forgive Rochester anything but what have I done?

KING: Mulgrave, would you be so kind as to escort Lady Castlemaine from the grounds?

BARBARA: That won't be necessary. I take my leave of you. (*Curtsies insolently to the QUEEN.*) Your Royal Highness (*To the KING.*) Your Majesty. Enjoy your next whore.

BARBARA exits.

KING: She's gone now Catharine.

The QUEEN sits on the floor and quietly sobs. The KING puts a hand on her shoulder but she flinches away.

Things will be different now.

BURNET has entered unobtrusively.

BURNET: Your Majesty, you asked to see me.

KING: Burnet, yes, I want to know what you mean by this. (*The letter.*)

BURNET: I see you received my letter.

KING: Yes, and I want to know what you mean by it.

BURNET: I mean what is written. No more and no less.

KING: You call on me to repent! You call on your King to repent of his 'licentious example to my subjects'?

BURNET: I merely report the appeal made by a former mistress of yours in her personal renunciation of her former wicked life.

KING: Jane Roberts has her own reasons for saying what she has said.

BURNET: Her repentance is heartfelt.

KING: She is marrying the Earl of Richmond. A very elderly but very wealthy man. This renunciation of hers is clearly a condition of her prospective husband who wishes to avoid the impression that he is being taken for a fool.

BURNET: Mistress Roberts was, before she came to court, renowned for her chastity. After she came here and was corrupted – I hesitate to say it but it is true – by your influence, she was renowned for being a harlot.

KING: She was never a harlot. Jane did what she did because it gave her pleasure.

BURNET: She tells me that she repents entirely of her many sins, embraces Christ and sincerely hopes that word of her repentance will prove an inspiration to others. It was at her suggestion that I wrote to you the letter you now hold, requesting that you follow her footsteps along the path of righteousness.

KING: I'm quite aware Mr Burnet that this is how you make your living. That your reputation rests on your ability to sniff out infamous penitents and commit their weary platitudes to paper, but listen well: I know your game, and suggest you refrain from the imposition of your infantile tracts on me. I have better things to do than read this kind of drivel.

BURNET: I resent the implication that I do what I do for personal gain.

KING: And I resent the implication that I don't know how to run a Court.

BURNET: You will forgive me for pointing out that you have more than a Court to run: you have a country.

KING: A country of po-faced Protestants who wish to deny themselves and me any pleasure. My gift to you was to be to show you how to enjoy yourselves again after the years of hypocrisy and hardship. But you don't want it. You English are too comfortable with your hypocrisy to change. I accept my mistake in misinterpreting what you desired.

BURNET: I wonder what makes His Majesty so cynical.

KING: There was not one inch of cynicism in my father. He took himself and his divine role as the head of state entirely seriously. And, if you remember, he was executed by the people. It's the people and their representatives in Parliament who've trivialised my once proud office. Not me. Nevertheless, Mr Burnet, I note your criticisms once again. I thank you for them. I will endeavour to become a different kind of king.

BURNET: Your Majesty.

BURNET leaves satisfied.

KING: Mulgrave, you may inform Lord Rochester that he is banished. Should he be found with so much as a foot in London, he will be arrested for the murder of the actor Thomas Downes and – this time – left to rot in the Tower.

MULGRAVE leaves delighted.

Scene 25 – Morning sickness

Adderbury (afternoon): ELIZABETH, ANNE
ELIZABETH unpeels an orange but a wave of nausea overcomes her and she discards it unbitten. She puts a hand to her aching breasts and, at this moment, ANNE enters, catching her by surprise.

ANNE: You'll soon have much to occupy you.

ELIZABETH: More embroidery, you mean. And music lessons? All the joys of married life.

ANNE: I've heard your retching in the mornings.

ELIZABETH: Where do you think your son is now?

ANNE: He'll come when he is ready.

ELIZABETH: I don't want to be like you and wait and wait and never act, and raise a child alone.

ANNE: As a mother, you will quickly learn the virtue of patience.

ELIZABETH: Did you ever consider that it was your stubborn certainty and your eternal patience that drove your husband away?

ANNE: And what is it about you, do you imagine, keeps your husband away?

Pause.

ELIZABETH: You know he's banished?

ANNE: Banished?

ELIZABETH: So he cannot be at Court.

ANNE: Who told you this?

ELIZABETH: Your friend, Dr Burnet. For so superior a person, he has a keen appetite for Court gossip.

ANNE: What has he done?

ELIZABETH: There was a fight at the theatre and someone died. Dr Burnet didn't know the details. Or didn't care to divulge them.

ANNE: When did this fight occur?

ELIZABETH: It was weeks and weeks ago and I've heard nothing from him. So I will go to London.

ANNE: You cannot travel in your condition.

ELIZABETH: I cannot remain in this condition here. I will go.

ANNE: Why London if he is banished?

ELIZABETH: I don't know where else to look.

ANNE: But if he's banished from London, why is he not here?

Scene 26 – Pox

Poxhouse (afternoon): ROCHESTER; KING; Mme FOURCARD

ROCHESTER: I have the pox.

ROCHESTER, stripped to the waist, sits and sweats in a steam room. The KING (disguised again) takes a seat opposite him.

KING: That much is obvious…

Mme FOURCARD, the Poxhouse Madam, pours a cup of water over hot coals, giving the KING an eyeful of her expansive behind.

KING: …no-one comes to Mme Fourcard's for the views.

ROCHESTER: Aren't you hot in your disguise, Your Majesty?

Mme FOURCARD looks up, intrigued, but only for a moment. She leaves to go about her business.

KING: (*Stripping to the waist.*) I hope she is discreet.

ROCHESTER: In her line, she has to be.

KING: You were damned hard to track down.

ROCHESTER: You've banished me. I'm hardly going to advertise my presence a stone's throw from the Palace.

KING: I wanted to explain my situation.

ROCHESTER: I know your situation. The golden days of your Restoration are long gone. The people and, more importantly, Parliament – who hold your purse-strings – will no longer accept the excesses of your court when they are themselves suffering such economic hardship.

KING: I wanted to ensure you realised that your banishment is no reflection on the affection in which I hold you. And the memory of your father.

ROCHESTER: So desperate still to be liked?

KING: Barbara and Jane too have gone. There's no-one left to talk to.

ROCHESTER: Go talk to Parliament.

KING: Parliament!

ROCHESTER: The holders of the Royal purse-strings are now the holders of the Royal testicles. And their grip is tightening. Go talk to Mulgrave. Go talk to Burnet.

KING: Burnet is too busy promoting Jane's recantation.

ROCHESTER: (?)

KING: You've not heard? Jane is to marry the Earl of Richmond. To smooth her passage to respectability, she's repented publicly of her corruption at the hands of you and me. Burnet is quite ecstatic. I'm glad I've brought a smile to your face.

ROCHESTER: You have to confess that is amusing.

KING: I feel let down. I feel let down, if I'm honest, by the lot of you.

ROCHESTER: We are the victims here, of your experiment. We and poor Thomas Downes.

KING: It was your experiment. I merely gave it my blessing.

ROCHESTER: I lost enthusiasm for it long ago. You forced me to continue.

KING: I encouraged you to follow your own passions.

ROCHESTER: Tolerance and oblivion.

KING: Tolerance and, in particular, oblivion.

ROCHESTER: Did you enjoy it though?

KING: It was diverting enough, while it lasted.

ROCHESTER: Bollocks was it. You used us up.

KING: Self-pity does not become you Wilmot.

ROCHESTER: Look at me here: pinned out on your dissection board, all scab and putrefaction. You can pull me apart, expose my viscera to the world, but you've no idea how to put me or Downes or Barbara or any of us back together and make us fit to walk this earth.

KING: Go home to Elizabeth. Let her put you back together.

ROCHESTER: You've ruined me for her.

KING: She ruined you for me. You took your eye off the ball when you married her 'for love'.

ROCHESTER: Why don't you fuck off and leave me to sweat and take my medicine?

The KING dresses to leave.

KING: You're wasting your time with the mercury, you know. No evidence whatsoever that it does any good at all. The cure is ten times worse than the damned disease.

ROCHESTER: Fuck. Off.

The KING leaves.
Mme FOURCARD returns with a burning mercury salve, which she liberally applies to ROCHESTER's exposed torso. ROCHESTER grits his teeth as the salve burns his skin. Next, Mme FOURCARD wraps his upper body in bandages. ROCHESTER stands.

Scene 27 – Tavern

Tavern (evening): ROCHESTER; FANSHAWE; ELIZABETH; ANNE; DRINKERS
Helped by FANSHAWE, ROCHESTER wraps a cloak over his bandaged body and stands on a table in a tavern, extremely pissed, and holding forth.

ROCHESTER: 'Nothing, thou Elder Brother even to Shade,
   Thou had'st a being ere the world was made,
   And (well-fixed) are alone of ending not afraid.
   Ere Time and Place were, Time and Place were not,
   When Primitive Nothing something straight begot,
   Then all proceeded from the great united – twat.
   Something –'

DRINKER: (*Heckling.*) Do 'In the Isle of Britain'!

ROCHESTER: 'Something, the general attribute of all,
   Severed from thee, its sole original,
   Into thy boundless self must undistinguished fall…'

DRINKER: (*Directly competing.*) 'In the Isle of Britain long
   since famous grown –'

ROCHESTER: 'The great man's gratitude to his best friend,
   King's promises, whores' vows, towards thee they bend,
   Flow swiftly into thee, and in thee ever end.'

DRINKERS: 'In the Isle of Britain long since famous grown
   For breeding the best…

   ROCHESTER accepts defeat and joins in.

ROCHESTER AND THE DRINKERS:
   '…cunts in Christendom.
   There reigns, and oh, long may he reign and thrive
   The easiest king and best bred man alive.
   Peace is his aim, his gentleness is such,
   And love he loves, for he loves fucking much.'

   The DRINKERS cheer their appreciation.
   ELIZABETH by now has entered, having at last tracked
   ROCHESTER down.
   ANNE has accompanied ELIZABETH, but waits for her at
   the tavern door.

   'Nor are his high desires above his strength
   His sceptre and his prick are of an equal length.'
   And she that plays with one –'

ROCHESTER falls off the table and collapses in a drunken heap.
ELIZABETH goes to help him, not entirely successfully, to stand.

ROCHESTER: Elizabeth. Good evening. Are you in good health?

(*To the crowd.*) My wife, everyone. Elizabeth: my charming wife.

ELIZABETH: Come away from here John.

ROCHESTER: Away from where?

ELIZABETH: Come home with me.

ROCHESTER: Home?

ELIZABETH: To Adderbury.

ROCHESTER: But I hate the country.

The DRINKERS cheer their support of his sentiment.

Everybody hates the country.

ELIZABETH: This is not about the country. This is about your vows and your responsibility to your wife and family.

FANSHAWE: Madam, I regret to report that marriage does not appear to suit his character.

ROCHESTER: Marriage does not appear to suit my character, Elizabeth.

ELIZABETH: You pursued me, you stole me! And now you have me: tied to your name, tied to your mother in the country, while you spend all your time here with drunks and whores.

ROCHESTER: Marriage is the end of pleasure, youth, wit, virtue. The end of hope.

ELIZABETH: It is the start of companionship, of security, of love.

ROCHESTER: It signals merely the end of the pursuit.

ELIZABETH: I could have made other choices. Even His Majesty offered me a position.

ROCHESTER: What, on all fours with your arse in the air?

ELIZABETH: Yes, I do believe he had something of that sort in mind, but I declined his offer because I wanted you. I'm sorry I came.

ROCHESTER: You are forgiven.

ELIZABETH: You are incapable of forgiveness. That's your disease. Your father was oblivious to you and you won't forgive him. You won't forgive me for allowing myself to be banished to the country. Or your mother for being surer in her faith than she is in her love for you. Even the King, who often seems to love you as a son, you can't forgive for his weaknesses. Even God you can't forgive for not putting you at the centre of His Universe. All the hours you spend writing your bitter verses against the Court, against pride, against constancy, against mankind and refusing to acknowledge that there is hope in the world, that there is a future. Feel.

ELIZABETH takes ROCHESTER's hand and places it on her belly.

… I am to have your child.

ROCHESTER stares down at his hand on ELIZABETH's belly until she withdraws it.

ROCHESTER: Bringing a child into the world is saying 'I've no more life to live, you go ahead and live, I'm ready to die.' It's an admission of defeat.

Silence.

ELIZABETH: Go to Hell then, I am done with you.

ELIZABETH leaves. ANNE follows her.

Scene 28 – A beating

Outside Palace and laboratory (late at night): ROCHESTER; FANSHAWE; CHIFFINCH (unseen); MULGRAVE
ROCHESTER is outside the Palace banging loudly on the door. FANSHAWE cringes beside him.

ROCHESTER: Wake up! Wake up! I demand to see the King!

CHIFFINCH: (*Off.*) What is it?

ROCHESTER: Let me in! I demand to see the King.

CHIFFINCH: (*Off.*) His Majesty has retired for the night. I'm instructed to let no one enter.

ROCHESTER: What kind of King is abed before midnight?

FANSHAWE: It's a little later than that, I think.

ROCHESTER: Don't you recognise who I am!?

FANSHAWE: Since you are banished I question whether you should be drawing attention to your identity.

CHIFFINCH: I do apologise My Lord, but you are not welcome at this hour.

ROCHESTER: He doesn't recognise who I am.

FANSHAWE: You're not looking quite yourself, I have to say.

ROCHESTER is not throwing stones at the Palace.

ROCHESTER: I call on His Majesty to repent his wicked life!

FANSHAWE: He will not like that.

CRAIG BAXTER

ROCHESTER: 'He is despised and rejected of men! A man of sorrows and acquainted with grief! He was despised and we esteemed him not! For he was wounded for our transgressions...'

ROCHESTER is off. FANSHAWE trails behind.

FANSHAWE: Where are we headed?

ROCHESTER: I know another way in.

FANSHAWE: I hesitate to remind you yet again but you are banished.

ROCHESTER: I know.

FANSHAWE: If you're seen, you'll be arrested.

ROCHESTER: I know.

FANSHAWE: So what are we doing?

ROCHESTER: We're going to kick the merry monarch where it hurts.

ROCHESTER and FANSHAWE exit...
...and enter again into the KING's Laboratory, which contains his telescope and microscope.

The King's Laboratory.

FANSHAWE: You have an experiment in mind?

ROCHESTER: The experiment is over.

FANSHAWE: So what are we doing here?

ROCHESTER: He claims white light is a mix of different colours. Has he tried to convince you of this?

FANSHAWE: Most of it goes over my head, I'm afraid.

ROCHESTER: You mix together paints of different colours and you don't get white, you get a shitty brown. To say white light consists of many colours is like saying the World rotates about the Sun.

FANSHAWE: Everyone knows that to be true.

ROCHESTER: Science doesn't describe the World as we can see it. It breaks it up, distorts it, until everything is meaningless. Life becomes a series of moments – some of them pleasurable, most of them not – plucked out of the void. I blame His Majesty.

FANSHAWE: That doesn't seem entirely fair.

ROCHESTER: He's the one we look to. The promoter of this empty philosophy. I want to know how to live, without destroying. He wants to destroy everything.

FANSHAWE: He loves you. He's lonely and he loves you and you've made it impossible for him. It doesn't seem to me any more complicated than that.

ROCHESTER destroys the microscope.

ROCHESTER: Are you going to help me?

FANSHAWE: I'd rather not. This lacks wit.

ROCHESTER destroys the telescope.

FANSHAWE: It lacks subtlety. No one will find it at all amusing. Even I don't find it amusing. We should leave.

ROCHESTER: Why? I'm just getting started.

FANSHAWE: I think I hear the Palace Guard approaching.

ROCHESTER: Come to me my pretty suckstresses. Come to me. Come oh come oh take me now!

It is not the Palace Guard but MULGRAVE who appears, sword in hand.

ROCHESTER: Ah, the unmistakable aroma of freshly stirred turd.

MULGRAVE: You're banished Rochester. And this act of vandalism is another in a long list of outrages you have committed against His Majesty. I've no option but to enforce the King's will and apprehend you.

ROCHESTER: I'm afraid I've no weapon, so cannot offer you any decent resistence.

MULGRAVE: Then you are a coward.

ROCHESTER: All men would be cowards....

MULGRAVE tosses his sword aside and lays into ROCHESTER with his fists.

...if they dared.

ROCHESTER is too weak to offer any resistance and FANSHAWE can only look on appalled as MULGRAVE beats ROCHESTER more than is necessary merely to apprehend him.

Scene 29 – Appleblossom

Privy Gardens (day): KING; QUEEN; ELIZABETH
The KING and QUEEN stroll arm in arm in the privy gardens.

KING: This is our best time of year, I feel, in England. Do you like the apple blossom?

QUEEN: (*Reciting from memory in halting English.*) 'But of the tree of...knowledge of good...and evil thou shalt...not eat for in that day...that thou eatest of it thou shalt surely die.'

KING: It would be delightful to hear you speak verses from something other than the Bible. For a change. Something contemporary perhaps.

QUEEN: 'In the Isle of Britain long since famous grown...'

KING: (*Enjoying the QUEEN's joke at his expense.*) Perhaps not quite so contemporary.

ELIZABETH, heavily pregnant now, curtsies before them (not without difficulty).

Lady Rochester, this is a pleasure. Please, come up from your curtsy.

ELIZABETH: Your Majesty. Your Royal Highness.

KING: We've been admiring the blossom in the garden. (*Beat.*) Are you in town visiting your husband?

ELIZABETH: He's dying.

Long pause.

I'm told he will not last more than a few days longer in the Tower. I understand and support your reasons for keeping him there. He has behaved badly.

KING: He has behaved criminally, treasonably.

ELIZABETH: Yes. But he was a good servant to you, for a period, before he became unwell. I know this request is unreasonable. It is unjustified. It is probably in vain, but will you allow me to take him back to Adderbury with me?

KING: How can I do this when he has done all that he has done and not so much as offered an apology to me?

ELIZABETH: I can offer no excuse on his behalf. Except that he has done what he has done because he loves you. I believe he has loved me a little too and yet he has treated me with similar disdain.

ELIZABETH is overcome. The QUEEN steps in to rescue her.

QUEEN: You are to have baby soon, yes?

ELIZABETH: Quite soon now, yes Your Royal Highness.

The QUEEN takes the KING's hand and looks up at him.

QUEEN: I think it would be nice if she take her husband home with her. Don't you agree?
(*To ELIZABETH.*) If your baby is a boy, I think, you will call him Charles.

ELIZABETH: Yes.

QUEEN: (*To the KING.*) Yes?

Scene 30 – Deathbed

Bedchamber, Adderbury (evening): ROCHESTER; WYNDHAM; MONTAGU; ELIZABETH; ANNE; BURNET; FANSHAWE; JANE; BARBARA; KING; MULGRAVE
There is a full glass of red wine on the table beside ROCHESTER's bed.
ROCHESTER talks in his restless sleep, dreaming MONTAGU and WYNDHAM.

MONTAGU: (*Disembodied.*) I, Edward Montagu, do swear by Almighty God that if I die this day I will visit my friends and speak to them.

WYNDHAM: (*Disembodied.*) And I, Thomas Wyndham, do swear likewise, by God and by my prick and by everything I live for, that should I die this day, I'll come to you and speak the truth.

ROCHESTER: (*Mumbled.*) By your prick?

WYNDHAM: (*Disembodied.*) I hold it very dear. Wait for me, I will come to you.

ROCHESTER: (*Mumbled.*) I will come.

ROCHESTER wakes to the sound of ELIZABETH's screams of labour, which terrify him. Eventually they stop. ANNE enters.

ANNE: John? Your wife has delivered you a beautiful son. Shall I ask her to bring him to you?

ROCHESTER shakes his head. He's still delirious.

ROCHESTER: No. No. No. I cannot.

Time passes. ROCHESTER sits up in bed, weak but no longer delirious. BURNET sits at the foot of the bed, transcribing his words.

For the benefit of all those whom I may have drawn into sin by my example and encouragement, I have to the world this, my last declaration: that from the bottom of my soul, I detest and abhor the whole course of my former wicked life. I have been an open enemy to Jesus Christ, through whose merits alone, I, one of the greatest sinners, do yet hope for mercy and forgiveness.

FANSHAWE has appeared in the room during the course of this statement. He now applauds.

FANSHAWE: One of your very finest performances My Lord.

BURNET: Mr Fanshawe, would you even now attempt to draw My Lord from his last hope of salvation?

FANSHAWE: Seriously, you don't think he's saying this in earnest do you? He's doing it merely to spite the King and appease his mother.

ROCHESTER: I have instructed my mother to destroy all my papers...

FANSHAWE: (*Worried now.*) Surely not....

ROCHESTER: .. with the exception of the hymns.

FANSHAWE: You have been composing hymns!

ROCHESTER and FANSHAWE both laugh at the ridiculousness of this suggestion.

At least allow me to burn the hymns as well. It would be a travesty were posterity to remember you as a composer of hymns.

BURNET: Will you sign this declaration?

BURNET passes the document to ROCHESTER for signing.

ROCHESTER: Dr Burnet will be dining out for the rest of his life on how he converted the most infamous atheist reprobate of the age with the power of his argument.

BURNET: I would say rather the power of God's love.

ROCHESTER is gripped by a seizure. His fist, in turn, grips the freshly signed document in his hand.

ROCHESTER: (*Hoarse whisper only.*) Would you ask Elizabeth, please, to bring me my son.

BURNET: You fetch her Mr Fanshawe. I will stay with My Lord to pray.

ROCHESTER: God can wait, Dr Burnet. I need to make my peace first with Elizabeth and my son. Leave us?

BURNET is reluctant to leave without the document.

BURNET: Your renunciation My Lord.

ROCHESTER: Take it.

BURNET must physically prise the document from ROCHESTER's clenched fist.

You have what you need, now fetch Elizabeth.

BURNET: Of course.

BURNET exits triumphant with the signed document.

FANSHAWE: It's not the same at Court without you John. The satire lacks an edge, the wit: refinement, the revels: a certain energy. One day perhaps you'll….

ELIZABETH arrives holding her baby. FANSHAWE discreetly leaves. ELIZABETH sits on the bed and places the baby between her and ROCHESTER. The bravado he displayed with FANSHAWE is now dropped. He seems afraid.

ROCHESTER: They're here, Elizabeth: Wyndham and Montagu. I can't be certain but I think they've come to tell me what's in store.

ELIZABETH: There's no-one here John.

ROCHESTER: Forgive me Elizabeth.

ELIZABETH: By the look on Dr Burnet's face, you have God's forgiveness and so no need of mine.

ROCHESTER: I've behaved…

ELIZABETH: Impulsively? Insensitively? Foolishly?

ROCHESTER: Wickedly.

ELIZABETH: I can't forgive you. You've crushed my heart.

ROCHESTER puts his hand on the baby.

ROCHESTER: Don't let this one go to Court. The people there are brutish, whoremongers?

ELIZABETH: I know they are. I'll keep him with me always.

ROCHESTER: I'm afraid Elizabeth / of the deep dark pit,…

ELIZABETH: Don't be.

ROCHESTER: … Of losing all sense. Of nothingness.

ELIZABETH: Oblivion?

ROCHESTER: Let's have a drink.

ELIZABETH: I don't think that will help you.

ROCHESTER: Let's have a drink. Fanny left some claret on the table. Let's have a drink. Elizabeth.

ELIZABETH reaches for the glass of wine on the table. She puts it to ROCHESTER's lips and he manages just a sip.

ROCHESTER: It's good claret. You finish it for me.

ELIZABETH stares at it for a few moments then knocks back the wine in deep gulps.

ROCHESTER: Is it good?

ELIZABETH: (*She can barely speak.*) Yes.

ROCHESTER puts has one hand on ELIZABETH's hand and the other on the sleeping baby.

ROCHESTER: 'Since first my dazzled eyes were thrown on that bewitching face
Like ruined birds robbed of their young,
Lamenting…'

ELIZABETH: '…frighted'

ROCHESTER: '…and alone, I fly'

ROCHESTER & ELIZABETH: '…from place to place.'

ELIZABETH dares not look at ROCHESTER.

ELIZABETH:
'My rifled love would soon retire, dissolving into air
Should I that nymph cease to admire,
Blest in whose arms I will expire,…

ROCHESTER hand slips gently from ELIZABETH's.

…or at her feet despair.'

Silence for a moment and then, from the shadows around the deathbed, BURNET, FANSHAWE, the KING, MULGRAVE, BARBARA and JANE appear.

BURNET: My Lord Rochester is dead.

FANSHAWE: He was a great man.

JANE: He was a great man and a great sinner.

FANSHAWE: He flashed across the skies like a bloody comet…

BARBARA: …filling all who knew him with astonishment.

BURNET: But he repented at the last and set himself wholly unto God.

KING: Repentance is the final act of cowardice.

MULGRAVE: All men would be cowards if they dared.

End of play.

LATCHMERE THEATRE

Opened as part of the Gate Theatre in 1982 and re-launched in 2002 as a theatre dedicated to new writing and the new generation of emerging playwrights, the Latchmere Theatre has quickly established itself as one of the most dynamic and exciting new writing venues in London.

> *'The tiny Latchmere Theatre...is carrying the torch for new writing and developing an enviable reputation for spotting the potential of playwrights at the start of their careers.'*
> The Guardian, *November 2003*

Since 2002 the Latchmere Theatre has staged over twenty new plays by important new writers including Phil Porter, Ursula Rani Sarma, Jennifer Farmer, Ronan O'Donnell, Samantha Ellis, Glyn Cannon, Peter Morris, Trevor Williams, Said Sayrafiezadeh, Falk Richter, Anna Marie Murphy as well as new plays by more established playwrights such as Ron Hutchinson, Naomi Wallace and Fraser Grace.

> *'The Latchmere...consistently unearthing some of London theatre's most exciting new voices.'*
> Time Out, *April 2003*

Artistic Director	Paul Higgins
Associate Directors	Johnnie Lyne-Pirkis
	Phil Hewitt
Literary Associate	Matthew Morrison
Artistic Associate	Jennifer MacDonald

Nominated for The Empty Space Peter Brook Theatre Award 2003

Plays premiered at the Latchmere Theatre and published by Oberon Books include *Touched... / Blue* by Ursula Rani Sarma and *Stealing Sweets and Punching People* by Phil Porter. All Oberon Books are available from **www.oberonbooks.com**.